blue
rider
press

Becoming Grandma

ALSO BY LESLEY STAHL

Reporting Live

Becoming Grandma

The Joys and Science of the New Grandparenting

LESLEY STAHL

BLUE RIDER PRESS
NEW YORK

blue
rider
press

An imprint of Penguin Random House LLC
375 Hudson Street
New York, New York 10014

Photo credits
Page 36: © 1973 by Fred J. Maroon
Page 93: © Annie Leibovitz/Contact Press Images
Page 116: © CBS Photo Archive/Getty Images
Page 209: Ina Jaffe/NPR

ISBN 978-0-399-16815-4

Printed in the United States of America
1 3 5 7 9 10 8 6 4 2

Book design by Gretchen Achilles

To Taylor and Andrew

Contents

Becoming Grandma

Over the River and Through the Woods

Becoming a grandmother turns the page. Line by line you are rewritten. You are tilted off your old center, spun onto new turf. There's a faint scent of déjà vu from when you raised your own children, but this place feels freer. Here you rediscover fun and laughing, and reach a depth of pure loving you have never felt before.

Becoming a gran exhilarated me with a new purpose. The change was so big and granular and unexpected, I wanted to understand it. So I took out my reporter's notepad and a tape recorder and set off on a journey, a quest, to find out what was happening to me. Does it happen this way to all grandmothers?

People have said to me, "Are you nuts? Writing a book about being a grandmother? Telling everyone you're *that old*?" It made me feel I was going to out myself, break some kind of taboo, like Betty Ford admitting she had breast cancer.

The implication is that admitting you're an LOL is self-destructive. Did you know that LOL has two meanings? "Laugh out loud" is one; "little old lady" is the other, known in the plural as "lollies." Which is funny because Lolly is what my grandchildren call me.

But most of the grandmothers I met on my exploration said they felt strong, physically and mentally. Though one did comment, "I think I may be on my next-to-last dog!'"

Does being an LOL mean you bake chocolate-chip cookies and are otherwise doddering? Or does it mean you went to college and possibly graduate school, got a job, stayed in the workforce and are now a BOT—a "bright old thing"—with power and influence? More and more, it's the latter. As we've had the Age of Enlightenment, the Age of Reason, and the Age of Aquarius, there are signs that at the turn of the twenty-first century we're entering the Age of the Grandmother.

One reason is that there are so many of us. Baby boomer women alone (aged fifty to seventy) are forty million strong, and the vast majority are grandmothers. It won't be long before more diapers are sold for oldies than for babies!

You'll notice that throughout the book I refer to myself as a "baby boomer." Well, I've taken a literary liberty, because technically I'm a pre-boomer, born in 1941. But I see myself as a member of the BB tribe: I was influenced by the same music, politics, and turbulence of the 1960s.

We older women, with our strength in numbers and our MAs, MBAs, and PhDs, are moving into positions of authority and visibility, flexing muscles no one knew we had. Women over sixty are CEOs and heads of state. And in our government, look at who's at the pinnacle: Janet Yellen (sixty-nine), chairwoman of the Fed; former Speaker of the House and now Minority Leader Nancy Pelosi (seventy-five); Senator Elizabeth Warren (sixty-six). It appears that "getting up there" is the road to breaking the glass ceiling.

We're beginning to see the influence in our culture as well. Hanna Rosin wrote in *The Atlantic*, "Youth is no longer cool—or at least its hold on cool has weakened." As evidence, the beauty and fashion industries are turning to sixty-plus-somethings to represent their lines. Céline, for example, chose eighty-year-old Joan Didion as the face of its 2015 collection, while Marc Jacobs chose Jessica Lange at sixty-four. L'Oréal signed the sixties icon Twiggy, now sixty-six, to sell its new cosmetics.

When I started on television in the 1970s, I was told that as a woman, I would not survive on the air past the age of forty. I guess the thinking was that the sagging would sag the ratings. As time went by, forty became fifty, then sixty. Hey, fellas, I'm still here—in my seventies! Ain't it the darnedest.

Research shows that people of both sexes feel more comfortable with ambitious older women than with ambitious younger ones. I gained some insight into why when I met the headmistress of a private school in New York. She told me that she used to take much more grief from the fathers than the mothers. "The dads were always thrusting their wagging fingers at me," she said, "raising their voices, flapping their arms, taking me on."

But when she reached her sixties, it stopped. "I thought I had finally learned how to take charge of a meeting," she said, "that I had gained the kind of respect from the fathers I had always felt was lacking." But then she realized something else was at play. "I had lost my sex appeal," she laughed ruefully. "I came to see that it's primordial. That once a woman can no longer reproduce, all that sexual tension, the boy-girl thing, goes away. The contest is over, so men are more willing to take us at face value." She said it was disconcerting to realize she was no longer appealing in that way, but then again, her job got so much easier.

This willingness to more readily accept an older woman in a position of leadership must be a factor in the rise of Hillary Clinton, the poster girl of the Age of the Grandmother. There's also this: that a gran carries an intrinsic moral authority and by definition conveys a sense of warmth. No wonder Hillary tweets and talks about her granddaughter, Charlotte, out on the hustings.

Speaking of herself and Bill, Hillary has said, "We just go to stare at her. It is wonderful and silly at the same time." Practically every grandparent in the country who heard that thought, Hear, hear! The experience of having a grandchild is a common bond, a fundamental human experience that people share.

This new world of powerful older grandmothers is populated by the same women who were the "revolutionaries" of the late 1960s and early '70s. They (and I) invaded and changed the workplace, as the first wave to benefit from the women's rights movement. Now thirty to forty years later, they're in the vanguard of a new revolution, pioneers again, defining and developing a new way of grandmothering.

As I explored the subject, I looked into the biochemistry of grandmothers, the history, and the economics. Because my own experience was based on just two grandchildren, both of whom are still very young, I went on a "gran" tour, asking my friends, my colleagues, experts and Google to help me understand the emotions, duties and problems inherent in the new American grandmothering.

One thing I found out early is that most grans are besotted. Just when you think your days of falling madly in love are long past, you look down at that baby and find yourself in a rapture, going limp. Having grandchildren is why they say old people are happier than young people. And why, as my father-in-law used to say, this is a pretty ol' world.

ONE

Life and Death

It's never too late to have
the best day of your life.

Throughout my career, I worked at suppressing both my opinions and my emotions. I was out on the streets of New York on 9/11 and held myself together. I walked the alleys of Sadr City and once raced to a café in Tel Aviv minutes after it was leveled by a suicide bomber without allowing my fears to surface. I've asked embarrassing questions without embarrassment. And I've sat opposite mothers of dying children, teenagers who had been abused, and grown men and women who had suffered the indignities of injustice—without breaking down in tears or exploding in outrage. I thought I had become the epitome of self-control.

Then, wham! My first grandchild, Jordan, was born on January 30, 2011. I was jolted, blindsided by a wallop of loving more intense than anything I could remember or had ever imagined.

At the very same time, my mother, Dolly, was dying. It was a disconcerting conjunction, to say the least. Although she had spent the last forty-five years complaining of one illness after the next, it was now for real. She might not live long enough to hold her great-grandchild. In no time, my diligently buried emotions burst out like kettle steam.

Dolly had fallen and broken her hip, which set off her rapid decline. My husband, Aaron, and I were with her at the hospital when our daughter, Taylor, called from Los Angeles. All she said was, "They started." Aaron and I kissed my mother good-bye, assuring her we would call as soon as we knew anything. We drove to her house for our clothes and on to Logan airport to catch the next plane to LAX. Our only child was in labor, four days early.

On the plane I fought off waves of fear: Would the baby be healthy? If something went wrong, would Taylor have to give up her career? For months I'd been pushing away such thoughts, those grandma gremlins. At the same time, I reproached myself for leaving Dolly. Would she be okay until I got back? We hadn't had the kind of even-keeled relationship I have with Taylor. When Dolly turned ninety-three a few months before, I told her I never thought she'd live that long, and she said: "Well, you don't have to say it so regretfully, ya know." Her dig, meant to be funny, was a reminder of the old rancor between us. As we both aged and mellowed, we became friends; now it pained me to leave her like that, in the hands of nurses at the hospital.

When we landed, Taylor was back home. She had gone to the hospital too early, and now she and our son-in-law, Andrew Major, were graphing her contractions on an iPad. I was sailing out of body. I couldn't believe it: my baby—having a baby. How could this be? She was my special Taylor, calm and imperturbable as always. She was signaling that's what she needed from me. I would have to quiet my nervous excitement.

At five the next morning, Taylor and Andrew raced back to Cedars-Sinai Medical Center. By the time Aaron and I got there, Taylor was already in a "birthing room," which was spacious and light with a panoramic view of the Hollywood Hills. And yes, we *could* see the sign! Monitoring tubes dangled; a nurse bustled about. Taylor had already been given an epidural, so we would have no Murphy Brown wailing, though I doubt Taylor would've wailed even if she'd gone without. Histrionics are simply not on her emotional keyboard.

She seems to have been born with something called hyperthymia. Roughly translated, it means "perpetual happiness." I have a daughter who didn't go through the usual teenage miseries or years of hating her mother (I confess to both). We had no melodrama; doors weren't slammed. She was so even-tempered as a child, I was worried. "It's just not normal," I told Aaron. "She must be repressing. Her head'll blow off one day. She needs to see a child psychiatrist."

"What'll you tell him?" he asked. "'My daughter suffers from being too happy'? Are you kidding?"

Eventually I talked to a shrink myself, who assured me there really are people out there, including teenage girls, who are never moody. Imagine.

So Taylor's equanimity in the birthing room seemed normal. When the contractions accelerated, it was *my* stomach that churned: "Where's the doctor?" I asked the nurse, with an edge. "Why isn't he here?"

"Oh, we never wake up the doctor early on Sunday," she explained.

As Taylor lay in bed, uncomfortable but composed, Andrew,

Aaron and I followed her cues and forced ourselves into a state of artificial nonchalance. But we are who we are: just as I was about to let loose my pent-up anxiety with a bellowing, "Where the hell is the goddamn doctor?," in he sauntered, like a reporter meeting a deadline by seconds.

"You're doing great," he assured Taylor. "I've been monitoring you at home on my iPhone." Good golly. Look how far we've come from house calls. Now doctors treat you from *their* beds!

He walked Andrew over to the window to show the father-to-be his cool contraction app. They chatted and swapped other new apps like two friends in a bar until Taylor said: "Hey, fellas, over here. Isn't this my show?"

Fifteen minutes later, the doctor announced: "Showtime!" And asked, "Will your parents stay?"

To my disappointment, Taylor said no. So Aaron and I slouched off to the empty waiting room. It seems that many of the births at Cedars-Sinai are Caesarean, by appointment, something Taylor was offered but passed on. Doctors like their Sundays off. As far as we could tell, only one other baby was born in the hospital that morning.

We paced and twitched and checked our watches every three minutes like actors before the curtain. Aaron and I already knew that it was a girl, and that her name would be Jordan, a name beginning with J after my brother, Jeff (who died in September 1999). I'd gone with Taylor to several doctor appointments, had heard the astoundingly strong heartbeat at just ten weeks, and at three months I'd watched little arms and legs float and wiggle on the ultrasound screen.

We weren't in the waiting room very long before the doctor

appeared. "The baby's perfect," he told us. "Out in less than forty minutes. An easy birth as these things go."

We ran back to the birthing room to see Jordan for the first time, swaddled in Taylor's arms, a little bundle weighing six pounds, fourteen ounces. I thought: A whole new person, and she's mine. I was so pumped, my heart was on a trampoline. And there was my daughter, soft in a way I'd never seen. Was this my tomboy who wouldn't wear dresses? She was now a Giotto Madonna.

Andrew was stretched out on the bed next to her so they could pass the baby back and forth. A pair so suddenly a threesome. At one point Andrew took Tay's face in his hands and kissed her lips twenty times.

Andrew has a temperament as steady and unflappable as Taylor's. They had met when he was working for Rob Lowe on *The West Wing* and she was a production assistant at a small movie company called Middle Fork. Her boss asked her to hire a new assistant. Andrew applied. Taylor loved his looks—he's often mistaken for Tobey Maguire—and she thought he was funny, which he is. She especially loved that he could tell stories about *The West Wing*, her favorite television show. She hired him on the spot.

A few years later he found a better job as a television writer in New York. Taylor told him it was okay with her as long as he moved in with Aaron and me, which he did, living with us in our small apartment for more than a year. The first few weeks were inevitably awkward. When Aaron and I had plans for dinner out, for example, we would call Tay in LA to see if Andrew wanted to join us. She'd call him in his bedroom, which was next to Aaron's office, where we were waiting for an answer. She'd call us back. "Yup, he'd love to."

The crazy three-step communication system (we didn't want him to have to say no to our faces) didn't last long. Within a few weeks Aaron and I were feeling we had reconstituted our family with an only child. Well, almost reconstituted. I've discovered that no matter how warm the relationship, there's always a certain etiquette when you deal with an in-law, a trace of formality.

On the day of Jordan's birth, I loved him like a son. Everything was unceremonious and comfortable. Since he and Tay had come to the hospital early, I kept urging them to take a nap. They laughed and teased me—I guess it was pretty obvious that all I wanted was to hold Jordan. Have her to myself. I thought about what one of my friends who had just become a grandmother told me: "All I wanted to do was lick the baby's face!"

When it was finally my turn, I felt I was growing a whole new chamber in my heart. I nearly swooned, staring at her like a lover. I'd never seen anything so delicate and beautiful, so sweet, every feature perfect. And it's not that I didn't *see* her three chins.

This is what I didn't expect. I was at a time in my life where I assumed I had already had my best day, my tallest high. But now I was overwhelmed with euphoria. Why was she hitting with such a force? What explains this enormous joy, this grandmother elation that is a new kind of love?

At first I wondered if it was from seeing my child become a mother. Or maybe I was subliminally realizing the forwarding of my bloodline, that my DNA had transferred to the new generation. Was I hearing little cries of joy from my genes—"I am fulfilled!"?

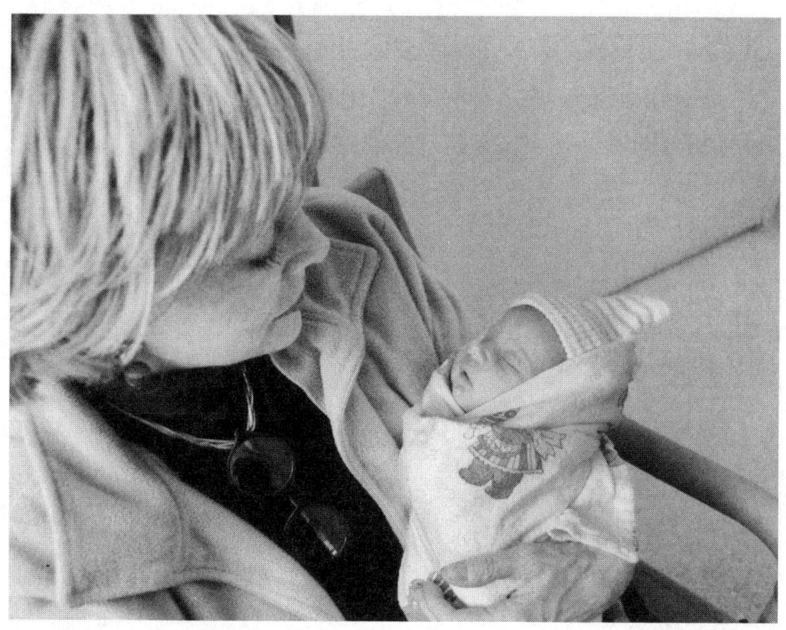

Meeting Jordan for the first time, January 30, 2011.

One friend told me that what struck her was that the seed of her grandchild was already in her daughter's body when the daughter was a fetus in *her* body. What an extraordinary thought, Jordan developing in Taylor when she was in my womb.

All I knew for sure was that I was in unknown territory. This was very different from the day Taylor was born. Hers had been a Caesarean birth, so for several days I was a woozy patient on serious drugs. It was Aaron who changed her diapers, wrapped her up in blankets, and walked her around the room. Now, as a grandmother, I was in perfect health, clearheaded, and not at all pleased whenever Aaron asked for his turn. What, hand her over?

When I did, reluctantly, Aaron held his granddaughter in the palm of one hand. This Texas-tall 230-pounder began blubbering soft baby talk. I decided it was a good time to call my mother, still in the hospital three thousand miles away.

"Jordan's here! And she's perfect!"

But Dolly yelled at me, snapping me into a different reality. "Get me out," my mother demanded. "They don't do anything for me here."

"What do you need?" I asked.

"I want to turn to face the door." But turning would put her on her bad hip. I felt so helpless. I tried again: "Dolly, you have a great-granddaughter." But she just continued to chastise me for

Aaron holds his first grandchild, January 30, 2011.

leaving her. This was a dark shadow on the day. My mother was unable to appreciate what she had so long yearned for.

Dolly had not wanted to be a grandmother. She thought it would mark her as old. But by eighty-five, she'd become what none of us ever foresaw: a sweet little old lady (most of the time). With her transformation came a craving for a great-grandchild. She wanted it so badly, she once hung up on Taylor when she had to admit: "No, Dolly, I'm not pregnant yet."

I, on the other hand, wanted to be a grandmother from the age of forty-five—when Tay was only ten. The tug for a grandchild was real and persistent. It made the arrival all the sweeter.

An hour after the birth, Taylor and Jordan were moved into a cramped single room overlooking a concrete wall. Jordan slept at the foot of Tay's bed, a collapsing pink balloon tied to her plastic bassinet.

Thinking up a name for her had been an ordeal. It actually started with a disagreement over a name for Taylor and Andrew's puppy. Aaron proposed Gilley; I was pushing Gertrude. But they wanted a strong unisex name and finally settled on Sydney.

When it came to my grandchild, the process was a long wrestle.

"I love the name Violet," I said.

"I hate flower names," said Taylor.

Aaron switched to cities: "Paris?"

"Paris Hilton. No way."

Aaron tried again. "Dallas."

"Dallas Major? Come on. It sounds like a stripper."

My turn: "I have a wonderful friend named Vijay. I love that."

"They'd call her Vagina."

I proposed BJ. "She'd be Blow Job."

Wisely, Taylor kept their choice secret until three days before she delivered.

Then there was the issue of what Jordan would call us. I told Taylor I'd like to be "Granny."

"No way" was her reaction. "It sounds frumpy."

I still liked it but was told that no matter what I decreed, the baby would call me whatever she called me. I thought that was nonsense. My mother wanted to be called Dolly, and all her grandchildren complied.

What if the baby tried to say my name? How would *Lesley* come out? Then it came to me: Lolly! It would come out Lolly—if I told her so. So I would be Lolly, and Aaron would be Pop. That's what he called his dad. We would be LollyPop. Cute, huh? Both Jordan and I had new names.

As a grandmother for only a few hours, I was enveloped in newness. I supposed I shouldn't have been, but I was startled when a lactation specialist dropped by. "Taylor, you're going to breast-feed? Really?" This was something neither I nor most of my friends even considered. We were in the first wave of women invited into the workplace under the banner of affirmative action, thinking we had to prove we could do our jobs as well as—and just like—the men. They didn't breast-feed; we didn't breast-feed.

With Taylor and her friends, it's a given. She had taken a class on it, but now, on her first try, she said, "I forget everything. Neither Jordan nor I know what to do." I was of no help. It did cross my mind: Thank God I didn't put myself through this.

The second feeding went a little better, though Taylor told me:

"It doesn't feel good at all." She was supposed to nurse twenty minutes on each side, but it took ninety minutes, since Jordan wasn't getting the hang of it, and Tay was wincing with pain. "She's given me a hickey already."

Jordan began to cry. "So sad," said Tay. "She probably hasn't had anything to eat at all."

Unlike tiger cubs, our babies are feeding incompetents in need of aggressive tutoring. The lactation nurse drizzled formula on the nipple to spark Jordan's appetite. That's when I congratulated myself once again for abstaining. I would've been a nervous wreck, which the baby would surely have felt and internalized. Ha! I thought. Taylor is calm and centered because I used a bottle!

I called Dolly again; her nurse told me she wasn't eating either.

On day two Taylor was in major pain and deeply worried about her baby getting nourishment. When she asked to spend another night in the hospital, I said good idea. The baby nurse wasn't coming for four more days, and Andrew was exhausted. When Dr. Laid-Back ambled in and slumped in the chair, Taylor complained that she couldn't get herself up and out of bed. She didn't tell him how inadequate she felt about the breast-feeding. In any case, the doctor said that since she didn't have a medical reason to spend another night in the hospital, the insurance would only cover one night.

"It'll cost you three thousand dollars to stay another day."

When he left, we decided to make up our minds late in the day. If Taylor still wanted to stay, Aaron and I would pay for it.

Whenever Taylor rested, I walked around the little room holding the baby or Aaron rocked her on his shoulder while Andrew snapped pictures. Jordan looked much better today. Her eyes were not as puffy. Were they swollen yesterday? Gee, hadn't noticed. I had thought she was perfect and gorgeous yesterday. Well, she was gorgeous and perfect that day. That's for sure.

A new lactation specialist, Deborah, came and stayed an hour and a half. It was just what Taylor needed, patience and tenacity. Deborah "trained" Jordan onto Tay's breast and showed how to pump the liquid out and breathe deeply to set up a rhythm. She taught Tay how to judge when Jordan was satisfied by how taut or relaxed her little arms were.

After forty-five minutes, voilà! Jordan was feeding. Deborah told Taylor this was much faster than most because she was calm, saying, "My other mothers get so tense. How does it feel?"

"It feels good." Jordan was slurping and Tay was triumphant.

Deborah said, "After feeding, put the baby's skin next to yours.

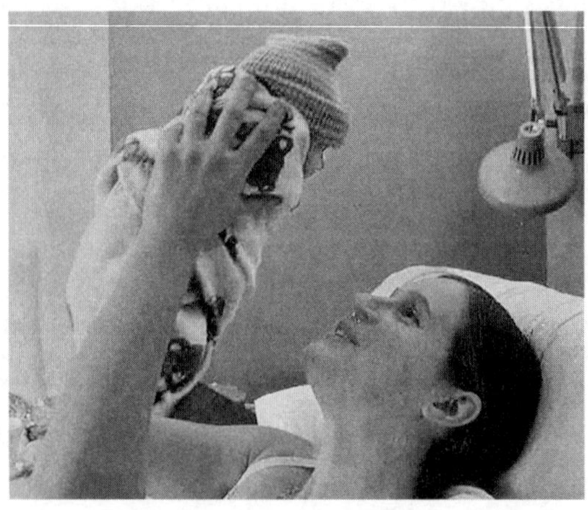

Tay and Jordan.

That's her favorite place on earth right now. Enjoy it, because in five years it'll be Disneyland!"

After Tay rested Jordan on her chest, she lifted her up against her knees and looked at her in such a tender way, I again wondered: Who are you? She kissed Jordan's eyes, then held her high in the air and just stared up at her. "You know," I said, "this is the first time you've ever played with a doll!" We laughed. It was true. "I've never seen you be so affectionate," I said.

"Andrew's changed me," she told me. "I married the perfect person."

Late in the afternoon, Taylor, whose favorite outfit as a kid was dark green overalls, put Jordan into a little froufrou dress. She had decided not to stay another night. So we packed up a dozen bags of diapers, receiving blankets, a diaper bag present from the hospital, adult diapers for Tay, a rented lactation pump, and Jordan—swaddled in a white blanket.

It took two cars to get everything home. Andrew drove theirs, Tay in the back with Jordan in a car seat, Aaron and I following in our rental with all their stuff. We stayed with them till ten that night, helping unpack, seeing to dinner, giving the two of them time to rest. With a newborn, you really do need eight hands. Only a few generations back, a new mother had a bevy of women around helping out: her mother, aunts and cousins.

In our hotel room the next morning, I began to wonder at the abrupt change in my daughter. This was the girl who preferred playing sports to tea parties and was scrupulously undemonstrative. Literally overnight she had mutated into a doting cooer. Was there an explanation, an article I could read? I approached this like a *60 Minutes* project, going online to dig around. The first thing I found was a reference to a book called *The Female Brain* by Louann Brizendine, a neuropsychiatrist. I pulled it up on my Kindle and read that personality and behavioral changes like Taylor's are normal in new mothers, because childbirth activates something called oxytocin, the mothering or bonding hormone. The sucking, the touch, the baby smell trigger the sprouting of what Brizendine calls "love circuits" in the brain. She says a woman is altered from within. It's like *Invasion of the Body Snatchers,* and it's powerful enough to change what even the most career-oriented woman thinks is important.

What I was seeing in Taylor was beginning to make sense. The hormones cause a new mother to literally become "addicted" to her baby. They also produce hypervigilance, a sometimes irrational fear regarding her infant's safety.

My reading was interrupted by a call from Taylor. She had just heard from the baby nurse that she had a cold and felt it wasn't a good idea for her to be around a newborn. The plan had been for Aaron and me to stay another night or so. I felt a need to get back to my mother. I was now her only child. Plus my unfinished projects at *60 Minutes* were piling up. But how could I leave Taylor and Andrew without any help? It was one of those either-ors that decides itself: Aaron and I would stay in LA. Together we would be the baby nurse.

I realized this was an opportunity to atone for the choices I had made as a mother. When Taylor was young, I was the CBS News White House correspondent, a demanding job that often had me working late or going off on trips with the president for days at a time. The nurse's not coming was a chance to make up for my maternal absences. What was to be one more day turned into a week and a half, during which I babysat so Taylor could get some sleep and I could get my Jordan fix. When Tay was nursing, she would get into a big, comfy armchair in the baby's room with something called a Boppy pillow—a doughnut for Jordan to lie on while she suckled. And I would sit with them in a state I'm not that familiar with: total peace.

Introducing Jordan to Sydney, their black Labrador, had to be carefully choreographed. Andrew had already given the dog one of the baby's onesies so she would be familiar with the little intruder's scent. When we arrived home from the hospital, we barricaded Sydney in the kitchen to keep her from the baby, all of us fearing aggressive sibling rivalry. Tay and Andrew had rescued Sydney a year before as a test, to see if they were nurturing enough to be parents. Until Jordan arrived, she was their spoiled only child.

When Andrew brought Sydney into the baby's room, she moved slowly. Taylor whispered soothingly as the dog edged up to the Boppy and sniffed. She then sat down and stared, trying to figure things out. Incredible. The dog seemed to realize this was momentous. How'd she know? She got up and went back for another whiff, lifting her nostrils up to the side of Jordan's head. And that was that. Satisfied, she lay down at Taylor's feet and went to sleep.

And yet I wouldn't say we were living in paradise. Jordan couldn't settle down after her evening feeding, so we all took turns walking her around. Did she have colic, as Taylor had? Aaron said it was too early to tell. But she did fuss and quiver with stomach pain. After Taylor gave her a sponge bath, Andrew rocked and sang to her until he finally lullabied her to sleep.

But all too soon it was time for another feeding. The nursing schedule was every three hours, for an hour. Taylor, *my* baby still, had a rash on *her* tummy, and her breasts hurt, so she was icing them with cartons of ice cream.

The next morning when I called my mother, she was more lucid. One of her nurses set up a computer for Skyping, so Dolly got to see Jordan for the first time, as she arabesqued her skinny little arms. Dolly was riveted. It was wonderful. But I noticed that her smile was crooked, and she was listing to one side. It occurred to me she may have had a stroke.

Later that evening Andrew's parents, Barbara and Roy Major, arrived and seemed to enjoy the same raptures over Jordan we did. They'd flown in from Kansas City for just a few days, both having full-time jobs: she a paralegal at her brother's law firm, he a drafting coordinator for a steel company. When she held Jordan, Barbara assumed the grandmother stare, that gaze of soft-eyed enchantment. Roy fell under the same spell. We kept passing our little baby around from Roy to Aaron, to me, and then to Taylor and Andrew and back to Barbara. Jordan was always in someone's arms.

This is another new territory for grandmothers. We find ourselves having to share the new center of our life with basically strangers. The sharing part can be difficult. Handing Jordan over to Barbara was wrenching; then again, passing her to Aaron or Taylor was hard too, and I know Barbara felt the same. The only time we willingly gave Jordan up was when she pooped. "Here, Tay! Andrew!"

I can only guess what it was like for them, as red-state, church-centered Missourians, having their son marry a blue-state-of-mind girl whose mother was on *60 Minutes,* with all that that implies, and whose father worked in Hollywood. But Aaron and I liked them immediately for their warmth and decency, and because they had given Andrew such wholesome values. The four of us spent the next few days giving Taylor and Andrew time to sleep. Barbara and I washed the dishes and swapped stories about being working moms and about our mothers. We found we had a lot in common.

On their second day in LA, I decided I could get a little work done, so I went to San Jose to interview John Chambers, the CEO of Cisco Systems, for a *60 Minutes* piece on corporate taxes. When I told him about Jordan, out flashed pictures of his grandkids. This was how I was introduced to the secret society of grans. We're instant compatriots. If you want to break the ice with someone who's in the society, all you have to do is ask, "So how old is yours?" This was actually used as a tactic during the 2015 nuclear negotiations with Iran. As the *New York Times* reported, one of the logjams was broken after the US nuclear scientist at the talks gave his Iranian counterpart gifts for his new grandchild.

In various surveys, nearly three-quarters of grandparents say that being a grandparent is the single most important and satisfying thing in their life. Most say being with their grandkids is more important to them than traveling or having financial security.

A few hours later, I was back at my post as baby nurse, having yearned for Jordan the whole time I was away. Now in my arms, Little Miss Dainty farted. Music! And pooped. Perfume!

To be honest, Taylor and Andrew performed most of the baby-nurse duties, like changing diapers and bathing. Aaron and I were more like the maid and butler. We ran errands, kept the pantry stocked, ordered and picked up takeout, and of course held the baby as much as we could. It didn't escape me that while Taylor was going through some kind of metabolic conversion into this über-nurturer, I was mutating into the hausfrau I had never been.

Hausfrau and supplicant. In a book of essays by grandmothers called *Eye of My Heart*, Barbara Graham writes that she felt as though she was auditioning for the role of grandmother. Yes. That's what it felt like. Am I doing a good job with the baby? Does my daughter approve? So while I was marveling at Taylor's sudden aptitude for mothering, I thought she was loving my loving her daughter. I thought I would get the part.

Ten days after Jordan was born, Taylor suited up, tying her daughter onto her chest in a Moby wrap, and took the dog and me out for a walk. I was leaving the next day, so as we strolled along, we discussed how she was going to manage her maternity leave without her father and me. Taylor and Andrew would be on their own. I begged her to at least hire a maid and suggested that, once she went back to work, she consider hiring a part-time assistant to help pay the bills and keep her life in order. I had just read an article about working moms who do all the bill paying, errand running, housecleaning, food shopping, cooking—and have no time for the baby.

Taylor laughed at me. "Mom," she said, eyes rolling, "I'll pay the bills and run my errands online on my lunch hour. I'll get things delivered through Amazon."

"Okay, okay," I said. I am so twentieth century.

Our last night in LA, we ordered a pizza and watched television, Jordan right there with us, propped up in a little rocker on the coffee table. I thought: This is the best of the best. I was filled with gratitude that Tay was letting me be part of it. Letting me help her. Love her. Hold the baby. Become a real grandmother. What a gift. I was *really* needed and it felt so damn good.

When Aaron and I landed in New York the next day, the first thing I did was call Dolly's doctor. Without much of a preamble she said, "Your mother has a lesion on her brain. It's a tumor on the right side, accounting for the weakness on her left side." It's why she was listing. "Your mother is near the end of her life," the doctor told me. "She'll sleep more and more now and just fade away. What she needs is palliative care."

I was numb. Shocked. My mother had cancer that had metastasized into an advanced stage. Eight years earlier, when Dolly was eighty-five, she had been diagnosed with lung cancer. I begged the doctor not to tell her. She would have been terrified. She was unaware all that time and had had no symptoms till now.

The doctor offered to help arrange for hospice care at home. After my dad died in 1994 my mother stayed on in their big house in Swampscott. I loved being there, looking out on the ocean. At night when the moon was bright it cast a path of diamonds across the water that danced right into Dolly's bedroom window. She would want to be there.

I kept thinking how cruel it would be if she never got to meet and hold Jordan.

When I hung up, I turned to Aaron. "I'll be an orphan like you."

"I miss Clyde every day," he said of his father.

"Do you miss the responsibility for him, the burden?"

"I miss everything."

The next morning I woke early with a heavy sadness. While I repacked my suitcase to go to Swampscott, I called Dolly's nurse, who assured me she wasn't dying. Not yet. It would be weeks, if not months.

Not only had I left my mother, I had also left my work at *60 Minutes*. Several projects were in limbo. So I decided to take a few days in New York to work—as I often do—on two or three pieces at the same time, including a story about Scott Brown, the Republican who was running for Ted Kennedy's Senate seat in Massachusetts, and the one on corporate taxes.

I was so stressed that night that I woke up at two a.m. worrying about organizing a funeral, dealing with my mother's financial affairs, selling her house. Then, with a pang of panic, I remembered she had given me the key to her safety-deposit box at her local bank, where she kept all her jewelry. I had no idea where I had put that key.

I woke up again the next night at two a.m., mad with remorse over not being with Dolly and frantic about the lost key. What if there was no way to access the bank box? Would Dolly's rings and necklaces sit there in perpetuity?

That morning Aaron and I were finally leaving to see my mother in Swampscott. As I was packing, an image came to me of my old green purse. It was like the answer to a crossword puzzle popping into your head a day later, out of nowhere. I found the purse, dug around, and there it was. The lost key!

When we got to her house, Dolly looked haggard. She was gray, her hair now just a few white strands. You could see that her left side was paralyzed. We helped her into a sitting position and got Jordan up on Skype. Taylor had dressed her in a pink onesie with monkey feet. Dolly touched the screen and smiled. I wanted to cry. My mother seemed like a little girl now. Mercifully, she was in no pain and still unaware she had cancer. Her mother, my dad and my brother all died of it. And now my mother.

Watching over Dolly in that beautiful house where I had grown up, I had time to think about my being a grandmother. This was a relationship I wanted to savor, and put ahead of the demands of my job or anything else tugging at my time and attention. I now had a new first priority.

But there was something more at work here, something mysterious welling up inside me. It wasn't that I hadn't been told that becoming a grandmother was the best thing that ever happens to a woman. But what I couldn't get over was the physicality of my feelings. When I got into bed at night, I would pretend I was holding Jordan in my arms. I was infatuated. Dare I say it? It felt like—ardor.

Was I, like Taylor, going through some hormonal changes? As I would do on a story at work, I found a phone number for Louann Brizendine, author of *The Female Brain*, and called her. She couldn't have been more gracious as I explained that I was trying to understand my grandmother feelings. Why, when I looked at Jordan and held her, I felt I was floating, that I was on a high. "I know it sounds hyperbolic," I said, "but I feel like a lover. I keep wanting to burst into song!"

She laughed but explained that in all of us the brain pathway for baby love is the same as the pathway for romantic and carnal love. "The baby brain circuitry came first. Sex piggybacked on it."

She said there's a good reason we use the same words for baby loving and eroticism.

So, I wasn't crazy, and I wasn't alone. Before she got off the line, Dr. Brizendine told me that when a grandmother holds the baby, her brain, like a new mother's, can also be drenched in the bonding hormone oxytocin.

Aha! There it was. We grandmas literally, actually fall in love.

TWO

Granny Nannies

This is the only time in our lives we fall madly in love before we know what the person is like.

—ELLEN GOODMAN

The First Lady's mother, Marian Robinson, was the First Mother-in-Law. She moved into the White House in 2008 to help Michelle and Barack with Malia and Sasha. The minute she did, there was David Letterman on her case: "A mother-in-law in the White House? Honestly? I thought this was the administration that was *against* torture!" So pilloried are we.

It does appear that *this* president gets along just fine with his mother-in-law, and, like a lot of working dads, *needs* her. During the 2008 campaign, when he and Michelle were constantly on the road, Gramma Marian stepped in and drove the girls to school, the Secret Service trailing in a separate car; she cooked them dinner, ran their baths and tucked them in at night. Marian became their granny nanny.

After the election, she insisted she wasn't moving to the White

House because "you just hear a little bit too much." She relented only after Michelle begged her "to help keep the girls grounded." That she couldn't resist.

So Marian moved into the third floor of the White House, one flight up from the Lincoln Bedroom and her daughter and son-in-law's. She continued shuttling the girls to and from school, took them on playdates, went to school events, helped with homework, and apparently lived up to a grandchild's view of "Gramma" as the softheart who thinks she's perfect, lets her eat whatever she wants and gives her total control of the iPad. Marian herself was once asked about her daughter's feeding the girls organic food and not allowing them to watch more than one hour of TV a night. She responded, "I have candy, they stay up late . . . and watch TV as long as they want to. We'll play games until the wee hours. I do everything that grandmothers do that they're not supposed to!"

Mrs. Obama said that the strict mother she and her brother had grown up with was body-snatched. "I'm like, 'Who are you? What did you do with my mother?'"

Marian Robinson came to love living in the White House. For her it wasn't the "gilded cage" Ronald Reagan used to complain about. Unlike the rest of the family, she was rarely recognized in public, so she often went to concerts and ran errands to the drugstore.

Marian had to improvise her role. In fact, most of us grannies today are finding our way on our own, since there are no role models for a grandmother in the twenty-first century. Baby boomer grannies are unlike grans of any previous generation.

When Taylor was born, Dolly and my dad came to the hospital, stayed at a hotel in Washington for another day, and that was it. When Taylor got older we would send her to visit them in Swampscott or to Aaron's parents in Spur, Texas (where it is said it's so dry, the trees are bribing the dogs!). But neither came to help. Taylor loved her grandparents and they adored her, but they didn't function as part-time nannies.

Growing up without a grandmother is not healthy for children. That's what all the research shows. Not that long ago, societies were structured so that grandmothers lived nearby, if not *in* the same house. It was the natural order, the way humanity evolved. Children were born into a family compound. While the mothers were out hunting or growing crops in a field, children and babies were left all day long with Gramma to watch over them.

Anthropologists have wondered why, in the Darwinian scheme of things, grandmothers even exist, why women live so long after we stop being able to reproduce. As Judith Shulevitz wrote in the *New Republic*, not only do older women take food out of the mouths of others in the family, "post-menopausal women lack obvious utility. They tend to be weak. They don't have much sex appeal." (Ouch.) So why are we here?

Well, it turns out there's something called "the grandmother theory" that offers an answer. Back in the Stone Age, older females foraged for edible plants for the family while they babysat. In so doing, they improved the health and nutrition of their grandchildren. University of Utah anthropologist Kristen Hawkes, who came up with the theory, says having grandmothers feed and watch over their just-weaned grandchildren allowed their fertile daughters to reproduce sooner, and more often. When grandmothers are involved in child care, young women are able to reproduce every year. (Well, some women.) Chimpanzees wait five to six years between babies.

There's even evidence that having a grandmother around can improve a child's prospects more than a father can. In one study in rural Gambia, researchers found that the presence of a grandmother cut in half the chance of a toddler dying. Whether the father was alive and present or dead didn't matter.

It appears that human grandmothers are one of the few animals on the planet that live long after menopause. Even the other primates do not survive much past their reproductive years. Jane Goodall's most memorable chimpanzee, Flo, lived well into her fifties, but she was fertile up until the end, giving birth just three years before she died. As far as we know, the only other mammals that live past menopause and are regularly midwives for their daughters and guardians of their grandchildren are whales, dolphins, and elephants who live in matriarchies, with the older females watching over the babies. How wonderful is that?

In much of the world, rural families still live in communal colonies with grandmothers and aunts raising the children. Novelist Bharati Mukherjee writes about growing up in India in a multigenerational household. When her parents married, as was the custom, they moved in with *his* family: his brothers, their wives and children, and of course his mother, ruler of the domain. She was Thakuma, Bharati's grandmother, an autocrat who taunted Bharati's mother every day for burdening the family with three daughters and providing no sons.

But while her mother was miserable, Bharati loved the compound. When she read about a girl in the West who had her own bedroom, she felt sorry for her. "How could she be happy if she didn't have scores of cousins to play with?"

As we humans evolved, grandmothers became the mainmast of the family. They improved the chances that offspring would survive and be fit. But in the last hundred years, people the world over have been moving from farms into nuclear-family apartments in cities. As we, particularly in the United States, became a mobile society and large numbers of women went to work, that tight grandmother link was loosened.

But today we baby boomer grans are retightening.

I have friends who move in to help their daughters for three or four months at a time. I know people who have picked up and moved across the country to live full-time near their grandchildren. In fact, almost three million grandmothers in the United States see their "job" as taking care of their grandkids.

Even if we don't, we go to the soccer matches and the school plays, and we take them on adventures. Grannies stepping in to help with the grandkids is becoming as American as taking selfies. You see it in the projects as well as the suburbs, with single working moms in Pittsburgh who can't afford a nanny and with well-to-do working couples on Park Avenue who don't *trust* a nanny.

If you're a grandmother who lives in the same city as your grandkids, chances are you spend at least one day a week with them—and it's the day of the week you can't wait for. My old roommate Carol Perlberger takes care of her grandson Oliver on Tuesdays, and another grandson, Syrus, on Thursdays. They call her "Nanny" and her husband, Ralph, "Abo," which is how Oliver first pronounced Opa, "grandpa" in Dutch.

"You should call your book *The Return of Laughter*," Carol tells me. She has a head of blond curls and an air of healthiness. "One of the greatest joys," she says, "is seeing how Ralph just erupts in laughter all the time." As she tells me this, she smiles, her eyes crinkle up and I think she has fallen in love with her husband all over again.

"What is it with a grandchild?" I ask her. It's early in my journey to understand the emotions. "It's such unconditional love on our part."

She pauses to think. "And they love us back! They love us unconditionally too."

I envy Carol because she lives within a few blocks of her grandchildren. She picks them up at school and takes them to either the park or a museum, or her apartment to play. And she's a wonder. She straps those boys on the back of her bike and zooms around the city. Or, in Oliver's case now that he's eight, she and Ralph take him skiing or to the beach. They're more like playmates.

So playmates with our grandchildren versus the policewomen we were with our own kids. With her two daughters, says Carol, "I was always telling them, 'Don't do that,' or 'Do it this way.' I'm not like that with my grandchildren. I never criticize and I listen more." We get to reboot with our grandkids, fix the mistakes and make amends for what we did as mothers.

"What I really love is that my girls watch me and say, 'Gee, she's so good with my kids.'" It's brought Carol a closer, happier relationship with her daughters.

However we do it, grandparenting is chapter four of our adult lives. The common view is that we turn forty, and that's it. We're fully formed—and don't change. But actually, when you're a grandmother, a whole new suite of behaviors unfolds. It's a developmental stage that has not been deeply examined as such.

I do recall a conversation I had years ago about how adult life is divided into chapters. It was with the great CBS News analyst Eric Sevareid. When I was first hired by CBS in 1972, I worked in the Washington bureau, where Eric would emerge from his office once a day. He was tall, with a handsome, chiseled face—the kind you see on Mount Rushmore. On his daily walk around the office, he rarely made eye contact, signaling to everyone: Don't even think of approaching for a chat.

But over time I discovered that behind that crust he was hiding someone shy and courtly. One night he spotted me working late and said, "Come on, Lesley, join me and a friend for dinner." His friend was Jacob Javits, the esteemed senator from New York. I was dining out with two of Washington's most respected wise men.

I don't remember the restaurant or what they ate—probably steak—but I do recall their advice, which was really more of a warning. Eric was divorced, and Jake's wife, Marion, was living

Documenting the Watergate scandal alongside chief counsel and staff director Samuel Dash and Carl Bernstein of the Washington Post *on June 26, 1973.*

back in New York. "Let me tell you about marriage," Eric said. "Like Gaul, it's divided into three parts." The first, he said, was fascination. Everything your new spouse says is adorable, witty, ingenious. You're enraptured.

"Just as the stardust begins to drift away, phase two kicks in," he went on. "You have a baby and together you think everything *it* does is adorable, witty, ingenious. And you're captivated. But when that wears off you get phase three: unrelenting, inexorable boredom." The two guys doubled over laughing.

Well, now we have a fourth phase, being a grandparent, and we're enchanted all over again. It's a whole new blossoming that comes with inexorable giddiness. Ellen Breslau, the editor in chief of Grandparents.com, told me that being a first-time grandmother is "like being a bride, with the excitement, the shopping, the elation." There are even baby showers today for grandmothers-to-be. This helps them stock up with baby monitors, sippy cups and Pack 'n Plays.

And there's the grandparent swoon. When we're children, our feelings are selfish; during parenthood, they're burdened with responsibility and fear, and lack of sleep. Grandparent love is unfettered, uncomplicated. Call it *ananda*, which is Sanskrit for "bliss."

This is especially acute with the firstborn grandchild. I was the first for my father's parents, and there was no question I was their prize, their reward. Grampa would bounce me, tickle me and laugh more than I did, like Carol's Ralph.

It was like what Ogden Nash wrote of the firstborn:

Stupendous, miraculous, unsurpassed,
A child to stagger and flabbergast,
Bright as a button, sharp as a thorn,
And the only perfect one ever born.

When my parents traveled, I was shipped off to Dolly's widowed mother, who lived in a small apartment in Boston. I would play with her miniature figurines or sit on the kitchen floor with an eggbeater, whipping up soapsuds in a bowl, as she made me whatever I wanted for breakfast, lunch and dinner. I don't remember her ever taking me outdoors. I thought she was ancient.

That's the way most of my generation saw our grandmothers: as frail, dusty with flour and very old. Though when you stop to think about it, they really weren't. We waited longer to have children, as have our kids. So actually *we're* older grandparents chronologically; we're just healthier and act younger. We don't play canasta in the afternoon, we go to the gym; we get blond streaks instead of blue rinse; and we're far more active with our grandchildren than even our parents.

Like my grandmother, Ellen Goodman, a longtime columnist at the *Boston Globe*, takes care of her ten-year-old grandson, Logan, when her daughter and son-in-law travel. But instead of Logan going to her in Boston, Ellen goes to him, several times a year. It used to mean traveling to Bozeman, Montana; now it's to a five-flight walk-up apartment in Brooklyn. The dragging up and down and up those stairs is a trek up the Matterhorn without a Sherpa. The worst, she told me, is realizing she can no longer bound.

Here's the thing about *being* older but not acting it: our grandchildren force us to confront what's lurking behind the bleached hair and faces puffed with fillers. As the old Gene Perret joke goes: "My grandkids believe I'm the oldest thing in the world. And after two or three hours with them, I believe it too!"

Over the summers, Ellen and her husband, Bob, take Logan to Maine with them, along with Bob's granddaughter, Chloe. It's just the four of them. No parents, no nannies. "When the kids finally leave," says Ellen, "I say to Bob: 'I'm going in the other room and I'm not going to speak till tomorrow. I'm friggin' exhausted.'" For those of us who waited until our late thirties or early forties to have our kids, there's that fear: do we have enough energy to be fun grannies?

On one of Ellen's trips to New York to see Logan, she and I had coffee in a hotel bar to catch up. We were bunkmates at camp. That's how far back we go. She's just the same as she was then—like my Tay, sunny and sweet-natured. She's also analytical and self-examining, and if you read her column, you know she's wicked smart.

Taking care of your parents, a sick spouse or small children, says Ellen, has a huge effect on your vitality and on your paycheck. "If you're a full-time caregiver, there's the element of exhaustion *and* financial sacrifice. You probably had to leave your job, so you lose an important part of your economic stability. And that can mean, on top of everything else, anxiety and fear."

But, Ellen adds, with grandchildren there is no weariness that competes with the elation and joy of being with them. She and I both feel there is something beyond the chemistry of oxytocin that binds us to these little fellas. It seems embedded deep in our genes.

When Jordan was a month old, I was concerned about Taylor, who was still sore and tired, doing all the nursing and housework herself. I called her and said it wasn't too late to get a baby nurse. "Why?" she snapped. "Don't you think I'm doing a good job?" I got my head handed to me. I'd never heard Taylor bark at anyone. I figured I overstepped, and backed off.

But then I couldn't help myself. A week later I asked, "Why not start adding some formula to Jordan's diet so Andrew can help with the early feedings?"

"When I feed her, the baby falls asleep on my boob," I was informed. "With the bottle, she gets wired."

I'm an idiot. Again, I withdrew.

She called me at eight the next morning (five her time), her old sunny self, to give me an update on Jordan and just to chat like girlfriends. I actually read about an analysis of nearly two billion cell phone calls and almost half a billion text messages showing that as women grow older, they and their daughters become best friends. Makes sense when you think about the shrinking generation gap: more and more we're sharing clothes, swapping career advice and Facebook likes. The study showed that as women age, their focus shifts from their spouses to their adult daughters.

Still, I was coming to appreciate that when our children become parents, the balance shifts. We grans begin holding our tongues. We turn passive, lest we irk or antagonize. We see clearly that they hold a new card, the power to deny us access to the most precious thing on earth. So we enter a new precinct of best behavior and walking on eggshells. We live by *their* rules now, and rule number one is: Do it their way.

A few days after that call from Taylor, I took the shuttle from New York to Boston to see my mother. In the last couple of years I had made the journey to Swampscott every other Saturday to take her and one or two of her friends (the ones still alive) out to lunch. I came to wish I lived nearby so I could see her every day. When I was growing up, she was the mother hawk who pushed me out of the nest and sent me off to live in New York. She wanted me to have a big life, away from our small town.

Dolly was propped up in a hospital bed in her own room. She no longer spoke in full sentences. All she could say was "Dress me" or "Get me up" or the rare "How's the baby?" At that point I got out my iPad and showed her a video of Taylor singing "Itsy Bitsy Spider" to Jordan. My mother squeezed my hand.

"Dolly, you sang that to me!"

After an hour or so she was dozing and never came back to full alertness for the rest of the time I was there. Just as the doctor predicted.

On the way home I got to thinking about granny nannies. These women have a more formal role than most grans, more like an au pair, only they're not employees, and they love their little charges with a champion intensity. Some granny nannies force themselves into their grandchildren's lives; others are there because they have answered their daughter's cry for help, like my friend Tish.

I met Tish (Alice) Emerson in the mid-1970s when she was president of my alma mater, Wheaton College. Later, when she was a consultant for other universities and foundations, she told me she was retiring and moving to Pennsylvania to take care of her grandchildren. I was stunned. It was the last thing I would have expected. Tish was an ambitious workaholic who had run a college while raising her two children as a single mother.

We met for dinner while Aaron and I were on vacation in Nantucket, where she and her grandchildren spend the summers. Tall with tightly curled hair and an incongruously high-pitched laugh, she is still fit, an avid golfer in her late seventies.

"My daughter needs me," she said. Her daughter, Becky, is a lawyer who works fourteen hours a day at a law firm in Philadelphia. She and her partner, Kea, who has chronic fatigue syndrome, have thirteen-year-old twins, Rosie and Spencer. Tish realized there was a chance to make up for all the hours she had spent at her desk and not at home when Becky was growing up. She decided to answer the call, as her mother had when Tish's kids were young. She says her mother set an example.

There were tensions with Becky when she was a teenager, she told me, and pinned it on her long hours at work. I told her what I told myself: mothers who stay home to raise the kids have tensions with their daughters too.

Over the years, Tish and I have had many talks about "balance of life" issues. As so-called pioneers, we're part of the have-it-all generation. But Tish was not in control of her schedule. Her days were long, and she was often on the road raising money for the college. I had Aaron to help me, along with a well-paid nanny. Tish was divorced and alone.

I asked if her relationship with Becky had improved. I have a feeling that Taylor actually loves me more now because I love her daughter so much. "Becky needs me," Tish said. "She's grateful—very. But I'm sure she's occasionally resentful because I'm a bigger part of her children's lives right now than she is. I'd be resentful too."

Becky is still the organizer, the majordomo of the household. Tish has adapted to her daughter's style as she tends to the twins from three to ten, three or four days a week.

"You're their Mary Poppins!"

"Sorta," she soprano-laughed.

Actually, she does more than your typical nanny. "I pick them up at school, take them to ice-skating, get them started on their homework, make them dinner, try to settle arguments and stop fights, clean up, do the laundry and put them to bed. Grandmothers have a larger role than a nanny and a different authority than an employee. I'm the enforcer. I'm like, 'No!' or 'Shh, not so loud,' or 'Show me your homework. You can't watch TV.'" So not *all* grandmothers are permissive Nana Candy Bar or Gramma Ice Cream Cone.

Tish has taken on the coloration of a parent; it is Becky who's the permissive one. "Working mothers—you may remember this," she said, "working mothers have a high need to please and be liked by their children. A *high* need," she said emphatically. "Well, a grandmother can be tougher."

"Really? I don't feel that at all," I said.

She gave me a what-do-*you*-know look. "Jordan's still too young."

"I don't think I'm ever going to be like that. I want her to love me."

"Just wait till Jordan's twelve or thirteen." There was foreboding in her admonition.

I asked whether she ever feels too old to be running after the kids. Tish surprised me: "It's actually helpful to be older. I couldn't do this if I weren't retired."

I told her about a couple I know who had picked up and moved across the country in their fifties, leaving their communities and friends behind, because they wanted to be in their grandchildren's lives.

"But isn't it also that they will have a child who's going to take care of them?" she asked.

"I don't know," I said. "I could see moving to be near my grandchild, but I wouldn't want Taylor to have to take care of me."

I got another what-do-you-know look.

"I decided to move to Pennsylvania as much to help my daughter as to have a child to take care of," she said. "For working mothers who didn't spend enough time with their children the first time around, this is a second chance." So it's not only a way to make amends, it's a way to compensate for what she herself missed out on.

She pointed out that we're part of the first generation of grandmothers who are not defined by our family roles. Having been those "pioneers" in the white-collar workplace, we have a professional identity. And yet, she said, we're the ones going bananas over our grandchildren. We're more like the men who were so involved in building their careers that they were all but absent from their children's lives. They end up lamenting their rationed fatherhood, so they go all in with the grandkids. "We're them," she said.

When it comes to child-rearing, there are swings from generation to generation about the best approach. What *was* trendy (spank 'em, give 'em formula) goes out of favor (never hit, only the breast). It's the nature of things, especially if you get to do it differently from your mother.

Naturally, some friction, some disagreements, are to be expected. The colliding and the squabbling are more pronounced when Gramma becomes the nanny and disagrees with her daughter (or daughter-in-law) over food and sleep, toilet training and you name it. Taylor's friend Ben comes to mind.

Ben was one of Taylor's bridesmaids (don't ask). He is what I imagine Ari Ben Canaan in Leon Uris's *Exodus* looked like. Tall and muscular, with curly black hair, Hollywood stubble and a wide, flirtatious smile. When I met him he was a struggling screenwriter whose day job was tasting and testing for the TV show *Fear Factor.* Insane as it sounds, Ben drank a "shake" of rooster testicles, ate a deer penis, hung upside down from a helicopter, and lay down in a pit with ten thousand emperor scorpions.

Fearless Ben met his wife, Huyen, while he was teaching English in Vietnam. He told me about the first time he visited her parents in their small village, Kim Bang, one hour by motorbike from Hanoi. To get there he and Huyen had to skirt the rice fields—with cemeteries in the middle of them—that surrounded Kim Bang. They drove down a tight alley and up to her parents' two-story house. "Her dad and mom kept touching my big nose to see what it felt like," Ben said, shrugging, with a smile.

After the wedding, he and Huyen moved to Jersey City and soon had a daughter, Shayna. In Kim Bang, new mothers stay in bed for weeks while female relatives wait on them. And my daughter was evicted from the hospital after only one night. Have we really progressed?

There were other ways life in New Jersey was a long way from Kim Bang. Maternity leave in Vietnam lasts six months; Huyen had to go back to work in three. That's when she asked her mother, Dung Zoon, to come to the United States to help. Dung Zoon got on her first plane and moved into a one-bedroom apartment with Huyen, Ben and Shayna in a rackety city. Ba, "Grandma" in Vietnamese, slept in the living room on a mat that she unfurled at night and folded up in the morning.

The culture clash began at once. Whenever Shayna cried, Zoon would sprint across the room, clap loudly in her face to distract her, and order Huyen: "Feed her. Feed her now!" In her world, they believe babies cry for only one reason: they're hungry, and when they are, they must be fed. Huyen told me that at home babies are fed every hour for the first three months. "That's why Vietnamese infants are so chubby."

There was constant skirmishing in the apartment. If Ben held Shayna on his shoulder, Zoon would lunge at him in a panic. "Stop! Lie her down." She believed babies shouldn't be upright for the first six months. "It's not good for their bones to sit up," she pleaded, genuinely afraid.

And she objected to diapers. In Kim Bang they train infants right away to pee (and poop) on Pavlovian command. They bring the babies outside, hold them out in front of them and go "Tsszzztsszzz." The babies learn to do their business on call.

Zoon stayed for two months—slowly, inevitably, yielding to our ways. It seems we won *this* Vietnam war. She began carrying Shayna upright and agreed that maybe disposable diapers weren't that bad an idea after all.

Despite all the scuffling, Ben and Huyen say Zoon was a lifesaver. "I loved my mother being there," said Huyen, "especially when I went back to work. I trusted her, completely."

You know you have a great job when they send you to Italy to work on a story about truffles, the most expensive food in the world. Aaron came with me, because it was Italy. We started the shoot in Spoleto at the Urbani Truffle Factory, where we learned that pigs no longer root for truffles. It's dogs now. Pigs got to like eating the great-smelling mushrooms as much as we do. In my case as much as I *did*. I'll probably never eat another one. Over the course of the trip, I had truffles shaved onto pasta, lamb, lobster, asparagus, polenta and, my favorite, baked potato. But enough is enough.

As often as we could, we would reach Taylor on FaceTime. You can be halfway around the world now and still be together. We watched Jordan sit in her little rocker at a table. Okay, we didn't get much back in terms of communication, but you're a grandmother and you think everything the baby does is adorable, witty and ingenious—even when all she does is sit. This long-distance, real-time hooking up does for grandparents what the pill did for women. It makes intimacy so much easier!

They say once you're over sixty, you don't know beans about technology. But we grans have a mighty strong incentive to learn. Anything it takes. Because even if we can't be with those babies, we can still share the big moments—the first step, first words, first bike ride, first ballet twirl, and first haircut. Some grans read books to the kids on iPads, and as the *Washington Post* reported, some are babysitting on-screen while Mom or Dad makes dinner.

Grandmothers are also tweeting, Instagramming, texting. And using Facebook. Yes, our grandchildren "friend" us even while they spurn their folks. When I interviewed Mark Zuckerberg, the founder and CEO of Facebook, for *60 Minutes* in 2007 (before I even knew what a social network was), one of the first things he talked about was using Facebook to stay in touch with your grandparents. "I actually have a couple games going on now with my grandparents," he said. "So they got on Facebook and we started playing Scrabble together."

A grandmother I met on an airplane told me that Skyping is helping her fight off loneliness. "When they're having dinner," she said, "you can be there with them." I wonder: do our kids really want us peering out through a tablet propped up on the dining room table every night? What about overstaying our welcome? But for grans who live across the country, or work full-time, or who just can't afford to visit multiple grandchildren multiple times a year, thank goodness for these new ways to see and be seen—in moderation.

I asked a friend what he thought it would be like in ten years. "Beam me up, Scotty!" he said. "Beam me up."

Our poor parents—those "phone people." Wouldn't Dolly and Lou have loved watching Taylor grow up.

"Look at her, so content," I said to Aaron as we watched our Jordie from Spoleto on the iPad screen.

Said Tay in the background, "We're giving her probiotics."

"What's that?"

"I don't know, but it's supposed to ward off colic. All the other mothers at the Pump Station swear by it."

I was curious about Taylor's circle of advisers, her working-mom friends who all seemed to operate by a strict set of rules. Call it child-rearing correctness. When I had Taylor, I didn't have a circle of advisers. I was one of the first network TV reporters to get pregnant, so in my world I was alone. It was still the era of schoolteachers being fired if they were with child. In my case, my bosses instructed the cameramen to shoot me tighter and tighter lest—heaven forbid—my ballooning bulge went out over the airwaves.

I read Dr. Spock, but only if Taylor was sick, and T. Berry Brazelton to make sure she was developing on schedule. It was formula from day one, Gerber baby food—and I drank wine while I was pregnant. Today I'd be sent to jail.

It wasn't long before I had company. Both Rita Braver, then a CBS producer, and Joan Barone, soon to be executive producer of *Face the Nation*, had babies—and diaper bags. We had no classes, no rules, no prescriptions. It was pretty much instinct and ad hoc. We were figuring out working motherhood on our own, as we broke new ground in the workplace.

Today the circle of working moms is much wider and the dos and don'ts more prescribed. Everyone breast-feeds and Cuisinarts organic veggies, everyone sleep-trains their little darlings under a precise regimen and gives them probiotics. They trade tips on the latest invention to save time, like fruit in a tube, and on the dangers of letting your child play with an iPhone. They are so much more diligent and assiduous about mothering than we were . . . than I was.

This uniformity is partly due to the Internet. There are a couple of sites young mothers routinely check in on, like BabyCenter or the Mayo Clinic. Taylor says they're her and all her friends' Dr. Spock.

One of the suggestions, from websites and her friends, was sleep-through-the-night training, something I was never told of.

When Jordan was five months old, Taylor announced they were going to give it a try. Aaron and I were on one of our regular visits to Los Angeles. At seven thirty our first night there, Jordan fell asleep in my arms and Taylor jumped up, yelling, "No . . . no no!" She grabbed the baby and hustled her off for the step-by-step ritual: a bath, followed by breast-feeding, and then into her crib. It would be the first time she'd have to fall asleep alone, not in someone's arms. "She has to learn she can do it," explained Taylor as the four of us sat in the living room, fixated on the baby monitor.

According to the training manual, you're to let them cry for three minutes, then five minutes, then eight, in intervals. In between, Mommy and Daddy go in the room and murmur reassuringly, "There there," or "We love you so much," but never pick the baby up. Several moms told Taylor it takes just three nights of this before they sleep through the night. We'll see, I thought.

Jordan screamed her head off for forty unbroken minutes. It was excruciating not breaking the rules. Aaron and I would have gotten Taylor after three minutes. But I said not a word. Didn't even squirm. I sat there totally impassive, nonjudgmental. And believe me, that was really hard. It took the weight of a bus in willpower.

Here's what's odd. Aaron told me later: "You kept interfering."

"No, I didn't," I protested. "I was the Sphinx."

"No way." Aaron laughed. He said that I was on their case constantly, saying, "This is too cruel," and "What a bad idea," and his favorite, "*We* never did this and you turned out all right."

I never heard myself! How could this be? I was so sure I had clenched my mouth shut the whole time. But in any event, they ignored me, and, said Aaron, they were happy to see us leave early for our hotel.

The next day Tay reported that Jordan woke up three times in the night but they didn't get up, and she put herself back to sleep each time. Night two: bath, breast-feeding, J into her crib, close the door, turn on the monitor and . . . what? She barely cried at all. She was fast asleep in five minutes. I was astonished.

A few nights later, Tay and Andrew went to see *Harry Potter*. As they left us to babysit, they handed us a sheet of paper with steps we were to follow precisely. Number one: Feed her at seven thirty. But alas, she was antsy and kept pushing the bottle away. We proceeded to number two: Change her diaper and put on her jammies. Number three: Read her *Goodnight Moon*. She tried to eat the book. Number four: Put her in the crib and sing "The Lion Sleeps Tonight." That's when the full-bore, red-faced hysterics started. We moved on nevertheless to number five: Tell her you love her, kiss her, turn down the light, turn on the humming humidifier—and leave.

We sat on the couch listening to awful guttural wails. We held hands as you might at a horror movie and stared at the howling monitor.

Item number six: Go in after five minutes. Tell her you love her again, but do not touch her. And leave. All of which we did, but she carried on and on. It seemed a month till she finally petered out. When I crept in to make sure she was okay, she was on her tummy, tush up in the air, fast asleep.

So it worked. O brave new world. I had no idea this practice has been around for generations. I thought about how much more engaged and eager-beaverly women today are about motherhood than I was. A young woman Taylor's age put it to me this way: "Your generation was all about moving into the workplace. It was a fight and a mission. You had to make it a big part of your lives. Our group, we're all like Taylor. We're more about doing both, but with more emphasis on our kids."

"It's a reaction to how much we took our eyes off our children, isn't it?" I asked.

She nodded. Of course it is. It felt like a rebuke. I had a lump in my throat.

Young mothers like Taylor choose to work. When mothers *have* to work, grandmothers are stepping in to help raise the kids in a variety of ways. In Latin America it is common for young mothers to leave their children behind with the grandparents while they work in the United States and send money home. They may not see their kids for years because they're afraid that if they cross back over the border without papers, they won't be allowed to return.

Here in the United States, young immigrants have to experiment with ways to raise children and continue working. Take Maura Pesantez, who grew up in Capareac, a small farm community in the mountains of Ecuador. She's five feet, two inches with a boxy frame and luxuriant black hair parted down the middle. She looks and acts like an assimilated suburbanite.

When she and her husband, fellow Ecuadorian Leonardo, had their first child, Henry, they asked Maura's mother, Lucrecia, to move here from Capareac. Lucrecia isn't like any of the other granny nannies I know. For the last ten years she has taken care of Henry and his sister, Sophia, as a real live-in nanny. Maura and Leonardo pay her a salary.

This has allowed them both to work full-time (Maura six days a week as a beautician, Leonardo as a carpenter) and not worry about the kids. Lucrecia, who still hasn't learned English, does the cooking and the housework and tends to the kids.

"I trust my mom," says Maura, "and I couldn't do it without her." But that doesn't mean there haven't been rows and run-ins. When Henry was born, Lucrecia insisted that getting wet was dangerous for both the baby and Mama. "If I did get wet, she told me I'm not gonna have milk for the baby," said Maura. "That meant no touching water for forty days: no showering, no washing my hair and no bathing Henry. Imagine." They were allowed to sponge down with a cloth dipped in an herbal stew Lucrecia cooked on the stove. That didn't last but a few days. But one of the running battles continues. Lucrecia often gives Henry and Sophia potatoes, rice and pasta—in one sitting. "I have to tell her, 'Okay, Mami, just one of those at a time. You'll make my babies fat.'"

But when the children get sick, Maura lets her mom use the old remedies from home: "I've seen them work," she says. If they have a stomach ache, "she will boil an eggshell with plain rice and the skin of a lemon. It really makes a difference."

As in most situations where young parents rely on Gramma like this, there are the inevitable difficulties. But in the end, Gramma is fulfilled, the children benefit from the love and attention, and the parents have peace of mind (for the most part). Everyone wins.

Of course, it doesn't always work out. There's the in-law issue, and the lingering-resentments-from-childhood issue, and the she-overstayed-her-welcome issue where couples find Grandma smothering or insufferable. Then there are the grandmothers who couldn't care less. They've been called glammas. One glamma told the *New York Times* that, like Marian Robinson, she would move into the White House, "but I'd hire someone to look after the kids!"

The first time I heard about the glamma phenomenon, I was fascinated, given my own over-the-top reaction to having a grandchild. I was at a luncheon when someone at the table volunteered that her mum was "less than nonchalant" about her grandchildren. When invited to come and see her newly born granddaughter, Mum said she couldn't that day.

"Why not?"

"I have a wax appointment," she explained.

"Come after," my lunchmate urged her mother, who said she couldn't because she had a pedicure after.

"You're joking," I insisted.

"Nope. Mum likes to swoosh in—and swoosh right out."

I wonder if grandparent enthusiasm is affected by grandchild order. This is something grandparents don't like to admit, but surely they find number one more interesting than number seven. I know of a man from a big family who was the last of his siblings to have a child. Sadly, by then his parents were over "the whole grandparent caregiver thing."

No matter the reason, a grandparent's standoffishness is often upsetting. Their sons and daughters take it personally. "My mother has never once offered to babysit, and she lives in the same town," one young mother told me bitterly. "'Did that with you and your brothers,' she says, 'and I'm done with it.'"

Interest in grandchildren can vary from year to year. But there are indeed women who are never interested. From my small sampling, it seems more prevalent among stay-at-home moms who feel they did their time. They love their grandchildren but have no interest in taking care of them. This is especially the case if a grandchild is born while Granny is still raising her own kids.

Then there are the grans whose image of being with the kids doesn't mesh with the reality. I work with a man whose mother-in-law says she wants to see the kids, but in less than an hour she can't get away fast enough. "To her, they're exhausting, boring and nerve-racking," he told me. "Even if we wanted to use her as a babysitter, it wouldn't work. Plus, she drives me nuts."

Another gentleman told me that when his parents used to visit, they fought so much with his teenage daughter that now when they come, they all move into a hotel—at great expense—so everyone has an escape route.

There are the grans who, instead of helping, add to the burden. A woman I met said when her in-laws come to visit, "they're beyond demanding. They announce they're coming for three weeks and all it means is extra work for me." With a look of exasperation, she went on: "And now they've announced they want to move to live near us. They actually said, 'So you can take care of us.'"

At five weeks, Jordan was old enough to get on a plane, and so Taylor and Andrew came to us. Tay wanted to spend part of her maternity leave in New York, sleeping in her old bed. There had been hell to pay when I turned her room into a guest room. Now I quickly converted it back to the way it was. I wanted her coming home with Jordan as often as possible.

Aaron and I prepared for their arrival by turning a small room in the back of our apartment into a nursery. We bought a crib, bedding, diapers, bottles, and a sweet bassinet I paid way too much for. When it was delivered—what on earth?—we had to figure out how to get the damn thing put together, with those screws and washers and that annoying little Allen wrench.

Aaron and I were both changed by becoming grandparents, but in different ways. I was a jitterbug, he a waltz; I was electrified, he was softened. We'd be with Jordan together, doing the same things with her, yet having different experiences. His loving her was every bit as deep as mine. His eyes would well up. But he told me he didn't feel that physical rush, that efflorescence of igniting spark plugs.

As a surprise, we went to Newark airport to pick up Taylor, Jordan and Andrew. They straggled into baggage claim with a stroller, a car seat, a breast pump and multiple diaper bags. I'd forgotten the miserable schlepping of baby travel. And there was Jordie, her little round face poking out of layers of pink blankets. She seemed so vulnerable. I grabbed for her, held her and made a noise. Donkeys bray, geese honk, grandmothers purr.

We moved them in, bustling and organizing. Tay fed Jordan in the living room, resting her on a wide, belted contraption called My Brest Friend, if you can believe it.

We fell into a routine over the next few weeks. After the early morning feeding, Taylor would hand off Jordan to me in the living room, where I'm usually up at six to read the papers. Now I got up early to amuse a five-week-old—not easily done—so Taylor could go back to sleep. This was just what I wanted: to be alone with Jordan and help my kid. I did have work in the office but managed to leave home late and get back early. It was like having an affair, I guess—cheating on CBS.

I'd sit with the baby in the mornings, and both Aaron and I would watch her at night so Taylor and Andrew could go out and see their old friends. We'd feed her, change her diaper, bring her into bed with us, then pass her back and forth making goofy love faces till she fell asleep. What we both wanted was Taylor to think we could handle Jordan on our own, that we knew what we were doing, that she could leave her with us and not worry.

One late afternoon when I was home alone with Jordan, she woke up crying. Walking her around did nothing to soothe her. So with her in my arms, I heated up the bottle of pumped milk Taylor had left in the fridge. But the feeding didn't help either; Jordan just kept crying. It was six p.m. and our black Lab, Parker, was barking nonstop. I put Jordan in her carriage and walked up and down the living room, picked her up, rocked her, but none of it worked. Just as it dawned on me that Parker's barking meant "Hey, you forgot to feed *me*," Taylor called. I did everything I could to muffle the noise, but she heard it all: the crying, the barking, even my frustration. She laughed at me and raced home. So much for building trust.

On the first Saturday after Tay and family arrived, we flew up to see Dolly for the long-anticipated introduction of her great-granddaughter. Again, the first sighting was a shock. Dolly was expressionless, bone thin and barely able to move. We couldn't miss the juxtaposition of Jordan's burgeoning life and my mother's slipping away.

Dolly was born in a caul. She always said it brought her good luck. And it is true she had a wonderful life, at least up until my dad died. For the next fifteen years she lived alone in that small town, her friends dying off one by one. It made me realize that the best place to grow old is a city, and especially New York City with its easy transportation and plays, museums, lectures, movies and free delivery of almost everything from tchotchkes to chicken soup. My mother spent the end of her life alone—and lonesome.

We laid Jordan on a pillow on Dolly's lap. She seemed uninterested, even with her great-grandchild right in front of her. Then my brother Jeff's family arrived: sister-in-law Paula, niece Liz and nephew Matt. They made a fuss over Jordan. Liz kept saying, "Ooh, I love her triple chin."

"Watch it," I said.

We all tried to pull Dolly into the moment. I had thought she was holding on, willing herself not to die until she met Jordan. But she seemed unable to comprehend that all her grandchildren were there, and that Jordan was the baby she had so desperately wanted.

A few days later when I called, the nurse said Dolly was weak, not eating, sleeping a lot. The nurse, Susan, put the phone to her ear, and Dolly said she was "okay." One word.

The next day Aaron and I went to a movie, *The Lincoln Lawyer,* and walked a few blocks to Fiorello's on Broadway for an early dinner. My cell phone rang. It was the nurse. "Dolly passed. It was peaceful," she said. Her last words: "Get me up."

Dolly's death collided in me with the freshness of Jordan's new life.

THREE
Natural Enemies

Of all the peoples whom I have studied from city dwellers to cliff dwellers, I always find that at least fifty percent would prefer to have at least one jungle between themselves and their mothers-in-law.

—MARGARET MEAD

Before I was a grandmother, I became a mother-in-law and found myself in a sorority much maligned and caricatured. Have you heard the one about how "mother-in-law" is an anagram of "woman Hitler"? Even Hillary Clinton once said, "I apparently remind people of their mother-in-law," and she didn't mean it in the sense of "What a lovely woman."

Before Taylor's wedding, Andrew and I were pals. I loved him. Would being his "mo'law," as he called me until I became Lolly, change everything? Would he come to see me the way Henny Youngman saw his? "I just got back from a pleasure trip," he said. "I took my mother-in-law to the airport." My God, we're a punch line. And a punching bag. We're seen as a posse of pains in the ass. Comedian Les Dawson said: "My mother-in-law fell down a wishing well. I was amazed. I never knew they worked!"

There's a pattern. Virtually all the jokes are told by a man about his wife's mother, when in real life the in-law antagonism is almost always between the women: a husband's mother and his wife. And from what I've learned, that conflict is all but inevitable.

Just ask my brother Jeff's widow, Paula. When they married, Dolly declared war. Even though Dolly had introduced them, she turned on Paula with a bloodlust. It hurt just to watch, particularly during Sunday brunches at my parents' house as Dolly ladled out her stew of insults and intimidations.

"Paula, don't bring food anymore. No one likes your cooking and your banana bread makes Lou"—my dad—"sick."

Once, Dolly invited an attractive girl to brunch and spent the meal asking Jeff: "Isn't Andrea beautiful?" "Don't you think she's interesting?" Ignoring Paula, she said, "Andrea, come sit next to me." Paula told me, "It was like she was fixing him up with her. It was so painful."

Shy, gentle Paula just took it. The browbeating was so merciless at times that my dad begged Dolly to "lower the flame," saying, "What if Paula withholds the children from us because of the way you treat her?" But even fear of losing her grandchildren didn't quiet my mother's out-of-control jealousy. This "other woman" had usurped her position with her son. How dare she.

And what about my brother? As far as I know, he never interceded, never told my mother, "Back off." I did. But all that accomplished was a week of Dolly's silent treatment.

Paula is in a sisterhood of millions. One friend's mother-in-law said in front of her: "If only Lennie had waited." It seems everyone has one of these put-down stories. In Italy almost a third of divorces are said to be caused by tension with a mother-in-law. In fact, the Italian National Institute of Statistics found that the chance of a marriage's lasting goes up with every hundred yards the couple can put between themselves and their in-laws. Sounds like one of those Henny Youngman jokes, but Italy's highest court of appeal has ruled that a woman has the right to demand separation from her husband if he fails to prevent his mother from "invading" the marital home. No joke.

From folklore to modern literature, the mother-in-law is portrayed as an ogress. It was a stereotype as far back as Roman times, when the satirist Juvenal wrote, "[There's] no marital peace . . . while your mother-in-law still lives." One of the most bloodthirsty tales by the Grimm Brothers is called "The Mother-in-Law," in which a king's mother instructs the royal chef to prepare one of the princes for her to eat "in a brown sauce." A mother-in-law with a cannibalistic appetite for grandson. Hmm. The story was so gory, it appeared only once: in the first edition.

Psychologist Mary Foote, who has both mothers-in-law and wives as patients, says that while every case is different, "the problem often starts with the mother-in-law expecting that her family's traditions and rituals will continue to be observed. When they're not, she can become difficult." It can start with where the couple is going to spend Christmas and Thanksgiving. And what kind of food they're going to have. "Don't underestimate this as a source of friction. It's huge. *Huge.*"

Even thornier, even more irreconcilable as a source of in-law conflict, is religion: If your son marries someone of a different religion and converts, your grandchildren will be raised with different values, in a culture foreign to you. Will you consider this heresy, a sin against your God? If your daughter-in-law isn't religious at all and raises the children as atheists, will you think that little Johnny is doomed to hell? This can lead to a fight for the grandkids' souls. One of the producers I work with at *60 Minutes*, Rich Bonin, told me that his mother, a devout Roman Catholic, was distraught that her grandchildren, Rich's brother's kids, weren't baptized. She consulted a priest, who told her that a layperson can perform a baptism in a situation considered an emergency. One weekend when she was babysitting, she decided that the children not having been cleansed of original sin was an emergency, and baptized them in the bathtub. She kept it secret for years.

It's not unusual for a husband and wife of different religions to avoid the disagreement by finessing the issue. Neither goes to church or synagogue or mosque. An inertia sets in, so that when children come along they're raised with no religion at all.

I know of cases where the young couple deceives their parents, assuring them that Tommy and Suzie go to Sunday school and church regularly. Jane Hartley, the US ambassador to France, and her husband, Ralph Schlosstein, told me that once when her parents came to visit, they all went to Sunday mass. Things were going along smoothly until their son, Jamie, said, "Look, Grandma. Look up. There's a big plus sign!"

Disputes over religion have led to children being disowned. The battles can become so fierce that marriages break up. More often, though, the grandparents suck it up. They give up the fight in order to see the grandchildren.

The cross-generational discord isn't *always* between the women. There are the occasional tensions between Gramps and the son-in-law, says psychologist Mary Foote, "especially if the latter makes more money. That can cause no end of problems." And it isn't always the mother-in-law who fires the first shot. Sometimes the belligerent one is the new wife, who is simply uncomfortable with her in-laws and withdraws, without explanation.

Far more often, though, the problem is mothers wanting to hang on to their sons. "In some families the son has filled in for what was missing in his parents' marriage," says Mary. "The son may have become her companion and her compadre. So then when the son gets married, the mother can't let go. And some sons are happy to stay in the golden boy position, leaving his mother and his wife to vie for him."

Nobody likes losing status or power. A mother-in-law is not only fighting for her son, she's trying to hold on to her perch as the paramount woman in the family. And while the mother and the wife battle it out, a man's self-preservation instinct tells him to hide.

Actually, it sounds a lot like the mother-wife battle over Franklin Roosevelt. Doris Kearns Goodwin writes in *No Ordinary Time* that "if Franklin thought that marriage represented an escape from his mother [Sara], he was wrong, for she was unable to back off and he was unable to make her go. Instead, he allowed her to compete with Eleanor for his devotion, . . . retain the purse strings for the family, and share with Eleanor in the task of raising their children."

Eleanor was oppressed by Sara's dominating personality, stung by her "belittling jibes" about how she comported herself, her wardrobe choices, even her posture. "If you'd just run your comb through your hair, dear," Sara once said in front of dinner guests, "you'd look so much nicer." Eleanor usually suffered the humiliations in silence, like my sister-in-law, Paula.

"There's definitely some hardwiring here," says Dr. Anna Fels, a psychiatrist in New York. "There's something in the competition for that man-boy. It's just built in." The new wife is perceived as breaking up the family, so the mother-in-law feels threatened. "Then the two women begin misreading each other, big-time. It wells up from their fears—or maybe they're intuitively reading each other's subliminal feelings."

"So what does the husband do about it?" I asked.

Dr. Fels said, "The son may have animosities toward his mother that he lets his wife express. The son doesn't intervene in any effective way because he's ambivalent."

There are all kinds of biological theories for mother-in-law hostility. In *What Do You Want from Me?* psychologist Terri Apter says that we humans have an instinct to protect those who carry our genes, and because the daughter-in-law doesn't have our genes, we feel an inherent resistance to accepting her, and she feels the same about us and our genes.

I was lucky. My mother-in-law defied the stereotype. Launa Latham was a working woman: a schoolteacher her whole life, an author and illustrator of children's books, a serious gardener and birder who liked to keep chickens and goats in the backyard. When I met her, her beautiful blue eyes were still clouded with sadness from the long-ago death of her twenty-one-year-old daughter, Von Sharon (Aaron's only sibling), who was killed by a drag racer.

Launa grew up in Spur, a small town in West Texas, the inspiration for her books about Gramma Prairie Dog's boardinghouse and all the critters (like the snake, Sam Rattler, and Mr. C.T., a cottontail) who come to visit in their boots and spats. She never lost her sense of fun.

My father-in-law, Clyde, was a flirt. Tall at six foot five, he was cowboy handsome. He actually loped in the boots he always wore, along with a bolo tie and a large, ornate silver belt buckle. Clyde held Spur High School's record for the most wins as football coach. Need I explain that he was the most popular and revered man in town?

Launa and Clyde were so different from my parents that understanding them at first was a challenge. There was some quality, a primary attribute that at first confounded me. They didn't act like any parents I'd ever known. Then it hit me: they were completely nonjudgmental. Aaron told me that when he decided to drop out of college in his freshman year and go to Europe, all his dad said was, "When should I come get your car?"

The Lathams were friendly and openhearted. Aaron once explained that they were like a lot of Westerners whose accepting nature had developed when people lived on isolated farms or ranches. Days would go by when they wouldn't see another soul. So when someone did stop by—even a stranger—they'd do everything to make them feel welcome so they'd come back.

Over the years I have met a lot of West Texans, but none as

broad-minded, as free of prejudice, as Launa and Clyde. They simply thought the best of everyone. And yet I was a nervous wreck around my mother-in-law. I had none of the typical complaints: she was never meddlesome, critical, controlling, disapproving. She was only warm and admiring. And still, I had a strong impulse around Launa to flee. This of course made me hate myself.

The most telling story about Launa involves the power of grandmother love. I met her ten years after Von Sharon died. Her sorrow was still palpable. She talked of her daughter constantly, in a soft, mournful voice—as if she was afraid to let the immediacy of her child fade. Then Taylor was born, and I watched Launa's suffering subside; her eyes sparkled again. Grandchild love is potent enough to mend a broken heart.

The image of mother-in-law as monster is global. In China it's ancient and intractable, often parodied in their sitcoms and dramas. By tradition the bride moves in with her husband's family. The poor thing is often treated like a slave by his domineering mother, the villainous *popo*.

But it appears this custom is on the wane as more young people move out of rural communities into big cities, where they inevitably live in tight nuclear-family units (a couple and their one child). Also, the new generation of only children is too spoiled and selfish to put up with it.

In India, Hindi soap operas are rife with mothers-in-law slapping their daughters-in-law around. Girls moving in with their husbands' families was the norm, and more often than not they were relegated to housekeeping drudgery, while the mean old crones took charge of the grandchildren.

Professor Vishakha Desai, former head of the Asia Society, says that "in much of India it is still assumed that when a girl marries, she will 'belong' to her husband's family." But she told me that as in China, those old customs are dwindling, especially in the upper classes. "Young women from wealthy families are ambitious. They work and have careers." But she explained that things are upside down. These working women expect their mothers-in-law to work for them, to tend to their children like nannies. "There's a certain sense of entitlement. She's working, after all; her mother-in-law isn't. So therefore, she should be there as the children's caretaker, even if they have paid help."

Vishakha says things are also changing lower down the economic ladder in what she calls the aspirational middle class, "where everybody strives to get their kids into a private school or to get a better car or to travel or whatever. And that requires two incomes." In this age of the Internet, this group sees what people in the West have and are doing and they want to get there themselves, right away. So now there's an expectation that a daughter-in-law will be educated and bring in that second income.

But cultural attitudes haven't caught up. "These young wives are going to work," Vishakha explains, "and they're bringing in money, but they also do the housework and take care of their mothers-in-law. That is the new version of the dowry system. The young women in this situation get creamed every which way."

"So the middle-class mothers-in-law are still in the driver's seat?" I asked.

"Oh yes. The keys of the treasury, the finances, are still with the mother-in-law. The daughter-in-law and the son who make the money are expected to give it to her. She manages the household and ekes out allowances."

There are some families in which the culture has changed dramatically. "Here's what I can hardly believe," Vishakha told me. "People in their late fifties, early sixties are giving up their lives in India to come to the US to take care of their grandchildren. Men and women. Once here they have no life outside of those kids. But they do it." Surely some emigrate out of economic necessity, but many others simply yearn to live with their family. Grandchild magnetism is universal.

We've had some cultural upendings in American society as well, with an inversion of the old dynamics of power. All I can say is woe to the mother-in-law who doesn't realize early on that once those babies arrive, it's the young wife who's at the controls. As psychologist Mary Foote, a grandmother herself, told me, "A mother-in-law has to think ahead if she wants to hold those babies. It's the mother-in-law who has to abdicate. She has to realize she can no longer be her son's number one love."

Most of my friends with grandchildren get this, and sit on it when they disagree with the way their grandkids are being raised. One friend's daughter-in-law is a vegetarian. "So the little guys eat tofu instead of ham and cheese," she says, "and I just kinda watch 'em."

Ellen Goodman, always wise, says, "I almost never open my mouth to criticize. All I open is my wallet!" If you want to see your grandchildren, you'd best do what she does and zip it. And right off the bat. "Don't get too involved in the wedding," says Dr. Foote. "That's where a lot of the animosity starts, usually over the guest list. And don't go to visit too often. And don't stay long. The kiss of death is the in-laws staying for a week in a small house. That's really pushing it. Mothers-in-law," she says, "need to be accommodating. The onus is on us."

"Not speaking your mind is the number one commandment," says author Anne Roiphe in *Eye of My Heart*, the book of essays by grandmothers. If you want to be invited to the birthday parties, don't offer help when not asked, and don't comment on *anything*. Not on food, bedtimes or discipline. "My poor tongue," she writes, "is sore from being bitten."

If you do slip up, the penalty could be devastating. I had dinner one night with a friend who opened up to me and described the agony of grandchild deprivation. This is a topic most women in her shoes prefer to keep to themselves, as if there's something shameful in being shut out of their grandchild's life: *Will people think I did something atrocious to be punished this harshly?* Twisting her napkin nervously, she confided that one day her daughter-in-law announced that "visiting hours" for the baby were between ten and eleven in the morning. Afternoon drop-bys would no longer be permitted. Getting to the apartment in the morning is almost impossible for her. She's beside herself. "What did I do?" she groaned.

I get the feeling that the closer the relationship between mother and son, the tighter the grip between them, the more the daughter-in-law will fight to loosen or even break that connection. The young wife needs her husband focused on *her* nest, not the one he grew up in.

Terri Apter describes how the tension can escalate: The daughter-in-law tries to establish boundaries between her and her mother-in-law, whose fear of being denied time with her grandchild is then intensified. Pushing back, she may defy her daughter-in-law, in which case the daughter-in-law puts on more limitations, which increases the mother-in-law's anxiety.

The cycle often starts when the daughter-in-law feels she's being criticized. Most new mothers are insecure. Anne Roiphe writes that the "vulnerability of a young parent [is] so enormous, and her confidence is so easily shaken . . . that critical words can be heard as an attack on her very soul. Challenge her competence and you strike at her heart. . . . It makes no difference if criticism is mild or serious; it will be especially painful coming from you."

Sometimes offense is taken when none was given. Say you, Granny, give advice. After all, you've raised a couple of kids yourself. But the new mother hears your helpful tip as "*I* know how to mother, you don't." Or you pay a visit and say—sincerely—"Ooh, I love what you've done with the room." The daughter-in-law might twist that into sarcasm. She thinks you hate what she's done with the room and then resents the phoniness. How do you deal with that?

Even an act of kindness can bite you. You straighten up a messy room thinking you're doing your exhausted, hardworking daughter-in-law a good turn. She walks in from work, sees the usual clutter of toys all neatly arranged and the dirty dishes washed and in the cupboard. That night she tells her husband, "Your mother slammed me today for being messy. I can't have her coming here anymore."

You've been silent as a Carmelite nun, but your daughter-in-law reads scoffing in your body language. One gran I spoke to said she does everything she can to ingratiate herself with her daughter-in-law. But then she added: "The thing that bugs me the most is she lets the baby have a pacifier too much." I'll bet anything her daughter-in-law intuits the disapproval. It's like they're reading invisible ink.

And then there are "the rules." A lot of us grandmothers have trouble with the new parenting codes. I suppose every generation comes under the spell of some new theory of what's best. But this group—Taylor's generation—follows a system few of us grannies get.

We probably did it all wrong. So many of us working mothers fed our babies processed fruit out of a jar, defrosted the veggies, and put plastic bottles in the dishwasher. Our daughters act as if we tried to kill them! After a full day at the office, Taylor plays with Jordan, then steams and purees broccoli she picked up on the way home. There's not a jar of baby food in sight.

My generation of mothers dealt with our guilt about leaving the kids during the day by being permissive when we came home. "Whatever you want" was our motto. That Tay and her friends are far stricter feels like a reprimand. It throws us off. "Don't you think she's being too hard on Jordan?" I've asked Aaron a hundred times.

A friend of mine organized a grandmothers' lunch at her summer house. Six of us sat outside on a lovely sunny day, sharing stories and laughing. None of the women wanted me to use their real names. This was a request I got from almost every woman I talked to about their daughters-in-law. I agreed to use made-up names; I don't want to be responsible for creating problems. Especially when avoiding problems is what these grandmothers are all about.

Melissa is a maternal grandmother. "I walk into my daughter's house," she says. "I just open the door and go in. Because it's my daughter's house. A mother-in-law can't do that."

That reminded me of a woman I'd met who has a daughter and a son. When she visits her daughter, she feels completely at home. With the kitchen arranged like her own, she feels free to make herself a sandwich or a pot of coffee while her son-in-law's walking around in his pajamas. But with her daughter-in-law there are barriers, a protocol. She wouldn't dream of going into the kitchen and just opening a drawer.

The six of us were all from Manhattan. The clean air and near-silence of the countryside and my promise of anonymity relaxed everyone into a state of candor. While we ate, Johanna brought up some of the new rules of child-rearing. Johanna was the one I most wanted to talk to, since I had heard she would do anything—*anything*—to please her son's wife. "My daughter-in-law has a rule," she said. "If I have picked up another child, I have to change my clothes before I can pick up my granddaughter."

"Why?" I asked.

"Germs. But guess what? I do it. I do whatever she wants. Everything, because I am scared of getting in trouble. I do everything."

"You really change your clothes?" I asked.

"Hazmat!" she says. "I change my clothes. George doesn't have to." George is her husband. Grampa. "He can do no wrong. He's perfect. It's only me that brings in germs. It's all me."

Everyone around the table was staring at Johanna with you're-out-of-your-mind looks. "I heard you built a new wing onto your house for the baby," I said. "Is that true?"

Johanna replied as if this were normal. "We're doing it right now. There's a hazmat suit in the new wing! I would do the marine crawl to have five extra minutes with the baby." She explained why so much ingratiation: "Look, I always want them to come to my house. I want them to travel with us. I just want that baby so much."

She said that if she ever steps out of line, her son pounces. "I say things to her like, 'Aren't I great? Aren't I the best mother-in-law?' And he says, 'Mom, shut up.' I have to be very careful."

"You're afraid," I said. "I see it in your eyes."

"I live in fear that I'll do something wrong. So if they say I have to wear pink, then I wear pink. Whatever it takes."

"Now, me," said Melissa, "I could work in the contagion ward of a hospital and come over and no problem—'cause it's my daughter. And yet"—she took a bite of mozzarella salad—"even though we have a fabulous relationship, I walk on eggshells with her too. If I irritate her over something, I'm afraid she'll say I can't visit as much. She could blackmail me." Yup, I thought, we're all hunkered down.

This was when Johanna brought up income inequality. It is something Dr. Anna Fels calls "a child trap," where wealthy grandparents buy houses with swimming pools and every possible amenity that a grandchild could want. Anything to get the kids to come over. It's the one advantage the paternal grandparents have—if they're well-heeled.

"If you're the mother-in-law, but you're rich," Johanna said, "you gain something." This introduces another set of potential complications, not with your daughter- or son-in-law, but with their parents. "It makes it difficult for whoever the other grandparent is," said Johanna, "because if one family can take the kids to the Caribbean or to Europe, it gives them an unfair advantage. It's an edge."

There's a natural jealousy toward the OGPs, the other grandparents, a jockeying for position, an urge to be the ones the kids like best or feel closest to. Ellen Breslau of Grandparents.com told me, "There's a lot of emotion when the grandmother feels like the other grandmother is the preferred one, that somehow she's the grandparent who's not as well liked, or she doesn't see them as much. Or maybe the other grandparents live nearby and she's the long-distance one."

From across the table Phyllis, who once worked in the White House, said this brought to mind a story about the first time George W. Bush met Vladimir Putin. The Russian president—who'd been taking English lessons—wanted to practice. "I read that you named your twin daughters after your mother and your mother-in-law," Putin said.

"I'm a great diplomat, aren't I?" Bush smiled.

Putin, laughing, said, "I did the same thing."

Bush responded, "Mr. President, you're a fine diplomat as well."

In some families it takes the diplomatic skills of a Benjamin Franklin. "Doesn't every mother and grandmother hope that her son or daughter marries an orphan?" Johanna said. We all chuckled.

A neighbor from down the street, Russell, had come by and joined us. He listened as Daisy, one of the grandmothers, said, "The loops and the hoops you go through. I had to get ten shots before I was allowed to go see our grandchild."

"Where were you going," Russell asked, "the Congo?" He turned to me and said, "I have the title for your book. Call it *Fucking Nuts*."

I wondered about Andrew's mother, Barbara. Did she feel she couldn't open the drawers in Taylor's kitchen? I screwed up my courage, and called her and asked if she was having a difficult time as the grandmother on the paternal side. "Please be honest with me," I implored. "Think of me not as Jordan's other gran, but as a reporter."

"Okay," she said. "I'll try to be honest about this." And she plunged in. "A daughter leans on her mother; a son leans on his wife." This would turn into an emotional conversation for both of us. "As the mother of the boy," she went on, "I feel left out a lot of times and I struggle with those feelings."

I had suspected as much, but hearing it from her directly put me in her shoes. "And," she said, "I'm especially afraid that Jordan won't know who we are." I felt a gust of affection and sympathy. She made me see that for her, being a grandmother is bittersweet merely because she's the father's mother.

"Do you feel resentment toward me?" I asked, practically whispering. I was afraid of the answer.

There was a pause. "Yes." Another pause, then: "I do have resentment. Financially, we can't afford to go see them often in LA. I understand that you can do that, and that hurts."

There it was. Out on the table. I've listened to many heart-rending stories on my grandmother quest, had women tell me things they said they'd never told before. Some have cried. I've teared up. But this was the most difficult interview I conducted. It was impossible to keep the usual reporter's distance, since the connection between Barbara and me is so central to both our lives. All I could tell her was that I understood what she was going through. If only I could have reached over and held her hand.

I hoped that it helped at least to clear the air. We went on to talk for nearly an hour, trading stories about Jordan. "When she arrives in Kansas City, she turns our house upside down," she said, "and I love it." She told me about the time she went to the Children's Museum and climbed up a two-story tunnel to retrieve Jordan (at about two), who had managed to get up the thing, but refused to come down. Once at the top, Barbara couldn't coax her back into the tunnel, so Grandma patiently stayed with Jordan for half an hour, "just sittin' up there," till Little Miss No relented.

Taylor is always telling me how patient Barbara is, and loving. She recalled the time that Barbara set Jordan up at her kitchen table with some paints, paper, cups and water. All Jordan did was pour—and spill—the water from one cup to another. Tay said that she and Andrew kept trying to get her to paint. But Barbara didn't care that she was doing it "wrong." She just loved watching her splash and spill.

An educator recently told Taylor that what Jordan was doing

was science. She was experimenting, learning by failing, which he said was the best way for kids to learn. "Parents and schools train kids to fear failure," he said, "which holds them back creatively." Parents are caught up in the outcome, "the product," while grandparents like Barbara, who think the grandkid's a genius if she puts her shoes on the right feet, love the process. They're perfectly content letting the kids learn by failing.

Once Eleanor and Franklin Roosevelt had their children, his mother, Sara, was more involved and interfering than ever. In fact, Doris Goodwin quotes her as telling the children, "Your mother only bore you, I am more your mother than your mother is." And Eleanor never disputed it. Indeed, she said of Sara, "As it turned out, Franklin's children were more my mother-in-law's children than they were mine." It seems that Eleanor was so unsure of herself as a mother, she all but abdicated the role. According to Bonnie Angelo in her book *First Mothers*, Eleanor was unable to cuddle and comfort her children, "a distance [they] never forgot or quite forgave."

Sara is usually portrayed as a villain, which Curtis Roosevelt, one of FDR's grandsons, says was untrue. He blames Eleanor (his grandmother) for creating the impression that Sara was an overbearing "dreadnaught." Curtis wrote that this was unfair to Sara, saying, "She never seemed domineering or aggressive to me."

His Sara was warm and fun-loving. On Sundays at Hyde Park he would get into bed with her and she'd read him the funnies. James Roosevelt (another grandson) said lovingly of Sara, "She was sort of a fairy godmother." She lavished the grandkids with money on their birthdays, took them on trips to Europe, gave them horses and cars. What the grandchildren called the two women says it all: Eleanor was "Grandmère," Sara was "Granny."

Here's something about Grandmère that caught my eye: she and her first cousin, Alice Roosevelt Longworth, Teddy's daughter, became rivals. Eleanor found Alice frivolous; Alice (famous for saying: "If you don't have anything nice to say, come sit by me!") took to doing bucktoothed imitations of her more serious-minded cousin. But while neither of them was what anyone considered an attentive mother, unlike Eleanor, Alice more conventionally became a doting gran.

With all the abuse from Sara, real or perceived, Eleanor never withheld the children from her. Denying a grandmother access to the thing she cares about most, loves most deeply, is in my eyes contemptible, but sadly it's not at all uncommon.

There are daughters with such a sustained rage at their mothers from childhood, they ration out grandmother sessions. But it's far more likely that the stingy gatekeeper of visitation rights is the son's wife.

Take my friend Mitzie, a widow. Mitzie is outgoing, exuberant, and as thoroughly American as you can be in every way except one: she's totally Italian when it comes to being a mother—a *mama mia*. She doted on her only son, Kevin, the way mothers do in Verona and Perugia.

I once did a *60 Minutes* piece called "Mammoni"—"mama's boys"—about Italian men as old as fifty still living at home with their mothers, who cook them whatever they want, do their laundry, change their sheets and even let them bring girls home for a sleepover in the same little beds they slept in as kids.

Mitzie's not like that . . . well, not quite. She's from San Francisco. When Kevin went to college in Los Angeles, she would drive down, slip into his dorm, gather up his dirty clothes and hide away in the basement laundry room while his socks, jockeys and whatever else washed and dried. She'd sneak the neatly folded clothes into his room, then drive back.

After college Kevin moved back to San Francisco, but not into his old room. He got married and had two children. "If I could have one person in my life back for ten minutes, it would be my mother-in-law," said Mitzie, "so I could apologize to her. When I would go away I would have my mother come up from Los Angeles to take care of Kevin, even though my mother-in-law was right down the street. Now my daughter-in-law does the same thing to me."

She tells me, her eyes glistening, that she's been put on a grandchildren diet, the visits parceled out like food in a prisoner-of-war camp. They live in the same city, but she sees her grandchildren rarely, and only by appointment. She has begged to babysit, to take them on outings, to have them sleep over, but she is almost always turned down.

"Kevin calls me when *she's* not around. He lets me come visit when she's out and he's alone with the kids. It's so tormenting."

One time the older boy got sick and went into the hospital. "Kevin said, 'Don't come to see him.' There was nothing I could do. I knew I couldn't just show up. So I said, 'Okay, but I'm going to send him something.' 'Don't go crazy,' he said. So I sent some books. Next day I e-mailed Kevin: 'How'd he like the books?' 'I didn't give them to him yet.'"

She goes on, clearly crestfallen, talking about the son she so adoringly raised. "He didn't allow me to talk to my grandson for two more days, and then I'm told what to say. 'Don't mention this and don't mention that. Don't make a big deal about the hospital.'"

She looks at me with incomprehension. This is a sophisticated woman with an important job in finance that she's held for more than twenty years. Being condescended to like that was unbearable. But she didn't argue. She'd already been broken.

"When I was finally permitted my one phone call to my grandson—I felt like I was a criminal—all I said to him was 'It must've been scary. You were really brave.'"

One thread running through many of these cases is the sons instructing their mothers on what to say and how to behave. In "When Things Go Tilt," one of the essays in *Eye of My Heart*, Clair Roberts (a pseudonym) writes that her son John told her, "Mother . . . you need to keep your *political* opinions, your *religious* opinions, *all* your opinions, to yourself. And you need to act your age." Roberts writes, "I thought he'd be pleased that his children are so fond of his mother. But no. My son was channeling [his wife]."

Mitzie and I were at a trendy restaurant eating fish smothered in Italian tomato sauce, something Mitzie probably makes better at home. She tells me, "I'm not myself around them. I tone myself down completely. I want my grandchildren to know the real me, but I'm constrained." This has been going on for five years, so long that she says she's gotten used to it. "The reason I'm not wounded and hurt all the time is 'cause I've changed my expectations."

I asked if she knew what crime she had committed, what infraction led to this cruel punishment of near-banishment. She has no idea. Admittedly, I have only one source on Mitzie's situation, but countless mothers-in-law whose visits with their grandchildren are measured out tell similar stories of being shunted aside "for no clear reason." They cannot explain the hostility.

The thing that still stings, she said, is that her beloved son has not defended her. She remembered an old *New Yorker* cartoon: two little boys are walking down the street and one says to the other, "I just broke up with my mother."

Denying grandparents access not only digs a gash into them, it hurts the children, depriving them of all that affection and belonging. At least Mitzie sees her grandchildren from time to time. There are cases where the occasional visit disintegrates to never, an outright ban, which can be like a sentence of a hundred lashes a day.

A businesswoman in Chicago I'll call N told me that at first she was not allowed to touch the baby. Her son explained that his wife had developed an irrational fear of her. Naturally this led to an argument, and soon N was prohibited from seeing her only grandchild at all. As with Mitzie, her suffering was compounded by her son's acquiescing to his wife. These are horror stories, making the mothers-in-law crazy, wondering, What did I do wrong?

I read about a study showing that when grandparents were denied time with their grandchildren, grandfathers developed symptoms of depression faster than grandmothers. The men's symptoms faded over time, but the women's lingered. It made sense to me: that a grandmother would never get over it.

Anna Fels told me one of her patients is considering going to court to see her grandchildren. Can grandparents sue for visitation rights? In some states, like Massachusetts, they can't; in others, like New York, grandparents can petition a family court. But if they win, they get monitored visits, meaning they see the children only under supervision. So the children may get the message that Grandma and Grandpa can't be trusted to be alone with them.

These forced separations can happen after a divorce or a death. It became almost a plague after 9/11. There were more than one hundred cases where parents of the men and women killed in the Twin Towers found themselves in contentious struggles with surviving spouses over the grandchildren—either because the spouse remarried or because of a dispute over money. The surviving parent tried and often succeeded in denying any contact. These grandparents suffered a double desolation: the loss of a child and then estrangement from a grandchild. Some of the grandparents obtained court-ordered visits. They got to see their grandchildren for four hours once a month, with a social worker always present.

Even worse than being locked out is the death of a grandchild. The pain is unendurable. Grandparents have their own suffering, which they must bear while trying to console their child, the parent, who is drowning in grief. The grans are often the ones holding the family together, dealing with the siblings, while attending to their son's or daughter's shattered heart.

After the murder of twenty children at the Sandy Hook Elementary School in 2012, *AARP The Magazine* interviewed several of those grandparents. Laurine Volkmann, six-year-old Jack Pinto's grandmother, talked of her agony. "We have been trying to cope with our own grief," she said, "but what hurts the most is watching Tricia [her daughter, Jack's mom]. She was curled up in a corner, shaking. I have never seen anyone in such pain."

Laurine's husband, Al, Jack's grandfather, said, "[I'm] grateful that I'm at the age I am, so I don't have to carry this sorrow with me for the next sixty or seventy years. But our children do."

As strained as my relationship with my mother often was, the idea of keeping her from my child was unthinkable. I recently watched a video of Dolly with Taylor when she was an infant. There it was, the all-absorbing grandmother gaze, the almost stupefied infatuation written on her face. And talk about playful! She was singing and dancing around the room with Taylor in her arms, laughing, calling her—as she would for years—Sparkles Stahl. She was consumed with love.

Not long after receiving the call that my mother had died, I shifted into my management gear. I contacted the funeral home in Swampscott, called the kennel about housing our dog, ordered plane reservations, spoke to Taylor about flying in, called the *Boston Globe* with the obit information and packed in a panic. I had no idea how I was feeling.

My sister-in-law, Paula, picked up Aaron and me at the Boston airport and drove us to the funeral home to pick out a casket and then to Dolly's house to choose something for her to be buried in. It was eerie flipping through her closet. We settled on lime-green pants with a matching silk teddy and a lime organza jacket with embroidered pink flowers.

I went to bed in my old room and woke up with the eulogy

Taylor and my mother, Dolly.

fully written in my sleep. I would tell Dolly's relatives and friends about how my mom had subjected me to a large dose of *Pygmalion*. I used to dread coming home after school. I knew I was in for another lecture. I think I got one a day. "Young ladies aren't loud," she'd say. I was loud. She wanted me to be proper. At the same time, she's the one who taught me to swear, introducing me to every dirty word in the English language. And some in French.

"You have to read more if you're going to succeed," she'd say. I was eight. She had plans for me, even then. Not having had a career, Dolly pushed me hard in mine. As I said, she wanted me to have a big life. And as much as I fought with her—which was often—I almost always listened. And obeyed. I would call home after I was on the air. These were exercises in masochism, like handing her a scythe to slice me up. She would home in on any mispronunciation or makeup smudge. She'd say: "We need to work on your hair. Go to Kenneth in New York. He does Jackie Kennedy." And "Take off the glasses. You can't communicate through those panes." She was the Marshall McLuhan of Swampscott, Massachusetts.

She had long instructed me to put my career ahead of family, saying outright, "Don't have children, they ruin your life." Yes, she said this—to *me*. But as she approached sixty, she wrote me an urgent letter: "I was wrong. You have to have a child—right away. You don't have much time. You're thirty-five. So just get on with it."

And you know what? I did. She had a way of making me do whatever she said. Even this.

At the end of the eulogy, I broke down when I said she had turned into a sweet little old lady. Afterward, I thought of what a wonderfully affectionate grandmother Dolly had been. She treated all three of her grandchildren with equal devotion. And they loved her back. It made me feel better that my mother lived long enough to know Taylor's story. She got to watch Taylor grow up and turn into a moral, responsible, kind person. She danced at Taylor's wedding, assured she would not be alone, and Dolly knew her genes were being carried on. I feel a twinge of sadness. I probably won't live long enough to know Jordan as an adult. Or

I might live long enough but not recognize her—like my own grandmother.

That night, Aaron played with Jordan. He has Parkinson's. He'd been tremoring and falling down, his face frozen behind a mask, his once-beautiful handwriting now close to illegible. He had all the symptoms. But that night, he propped Jordan up on his knees. "Giddyup!" he said, making her arms and legs dance. He laughed. She smiled back. It looked as though she was curing him.

FOUR
House in the Bronx

Somebody loves me, I wonder who.

—GEORGE GERSHWIN,

"Somebody Loves Me," *George White's Scandals*

Think for a minute about the grandparents you know. Whether they're living near their grandchildren or far away, whether they're college professors or plumbers, chances are they're helping out with child care. Young couples are turning to their parents more and more because, generally speaking, the older generation has the resources, with savings accounts, monthly pension payments, Social Security checks and paid-off mortgages. As much as 60 percent of grandparents are stepping in to help raise the kids by babysitting, doing homework, running errands or, at the least, giving money.

Then there are the grandparents who do more than merely help out or nanny a few days a week; they're actually raising the kids full-time. One in ten American children lives with a grandparent, and a third of them count on their grandparents as their primary caretakers. In some cases, the parents walked away, simply left the kids on *their* parents' doorstep (some because of drug abuse or mental illness). There's really no telling how many parents do that, just drop off their kids, and it's not always unmarried teenagers in the inner cities.

I heard Whoopi Goldberg tell Liz Smith, during an interview at a charity benefit a few years ago, that she left *her* daughter with her mother so she could pursue her career. Whoopi, born Caryn Johnson, and I were once business partners in a Web company called Wow-O-Wow, which stands for Women on the Web, but I hadn't known she was a grandmother.

When Liz introduced Whoopi, she mentioned all her awards—the Oscar, Emmy, Tony, Image, Grammy, Mark Twain, People's Choice—and noted that she was now a star of *The View.*

"*The View* has become the news-comment place du jour, as if you were Edward R. Murrow!" Liz quipped. "How do you explain that?"

"The dishevelment of society," said Whoopi, making everyone laugh, which she—in black pants, sneakers, and her trademark dreadlocks—did repeatedly. But the meat of the discussion was serious: about her resilience in overcoming, as Liz put it, her dark and stormy life. "You didn't graduate from high school. You were dyslexic." As Liz marched through the storms of Whoopi's early years when she was being raised by a single mom, Whoopi was clearly uncomfortable. "Forgive me," she interrupted, "but this is like getting my period again, having to talk about this kinda stuff. It's horrifying."

Ignoring her discomfort—as any good interviewer would—Liz continued on about Whoopi's years of adversity to underscore just how resilient she's been. "You've worked in your time in a funeral parlor, as a dishwasher, a bricklayer."

"I was a mason. Still am a mason." She smiled, all perky. "And a hairdresser—I have a license. So I can cut your hair and help build your house!" Then she became reflective and said that when her career finally took off, she turned the raising of her then ten-year-old daughter, Alexandrea, over to her mom.

A few weeks after the Liz Smith event, I called Whoopi and asked for an interview. Tape recorder in hand, I met up with her at *The View*. Her expressions, her posture, even her office made me smile. In a corner nook, the walls are floor-to-ceiling bookcases filled not with books, but with shoes. Sneakers, boots, platform espadrilles, pumps, open-toes, sling-backs, slippers, sandals—in different fabrics and skins and, it seemed, every color Crayola ever made. It was there that I, so incongruously, asked what happened with her daughter.

She told me she was living in Berkeley, raising Alexandrea, when her big break came. "It was everything I ever wanted and worked so hard for, and it was being handed to me on a silver platter." She had been doing stand-up routines at comedy clubs on the Strip in Los Angeles, developing *Spook Show*, in which she played different characters, like a blond Valley girl. Word spread, and soon she was performing in New York, where Mike Nichols saw her and offered her a one-person show on Broadway. That led to a call from Steven Spielberg and a role in *The Color Purple*. She was galloping out the gate.

"I should've said, 'No, no, I'm going to raise my kid.' But I wanted it—the career. I knew if I was going to do anything, now was the time to strike." So she called her mother and asked her to move out to Berkeley from Harlem. "All she said was, 'When do you need me?' and she was on a plane, like boom." Alexandrea was her only grandchild. I thought: of course she jumped.

"Did she ever make you feel guilty for leaving your child?"

"Not for one second. She wouldn't let me feel bad about this."

But there's no question it weighed on Whoopi's conscience. "I just left." She was leaning forward, looking down. "I wasn't a good parent. I left my child. I get it. I wasn't there for her birthdays: eleventh, twelfth, thirteenth. But I was able to provide for her and give her a better life."

It seems that the money wasn't enough for Alexandrea. She was a teenager, angry with her mother for not being there. "And so," said Whoopi, "she acted out. My kid got pregnant at fourteen. 'What do you want to do?' I asked her. 'I want to have it. I want to keep the baby.'"

Whoopi told me she thought that would be a mistake. "She was a baby herself. But my mother sided with Alexandrea. 'Aren't you the one always marching for choice?' she said. 'This is her choice and we're lucky we can do this with her.'"

So Whoopi's mother, Emma, helped raise Alexandrea and the new baby, Amarah, her great-grandchild. The family dynamic was skillfully captured by the great Annie Leibovitz in her evocative black-and-white photograph of four generations: Grandma Emma is focused on the new baby; Whoopi is looking out at us, her audience.

Years later, Whoopi asked her daughter why she had wanted the baby and she said, "I wanted to have somebody who didn't know you."

"That was hard to hear," Whoopi told me. "But I got it. It's hard to be the kid of a famous person."

When Whoopi became a grandmother, it wasn't easy for her.

She was just thirty-three years old. "You look in the mirror. 'Wow, I'm somebody's grandmother.' It was freaky."

And yet when she tells me about Alexandrea's baby, Whoopi sounds like every other hopelessly gaga grandma. "When my granddaughter, Amarah Skye, was born, from the first time I saw

Whoopi Goldberg with her mother, Emma Johnson, daughter Alexandrea Martin, and granddaughter Amarah Skye, 1989.

her, there was something about her. She took to me and I took to her." I thought she was going to quote *Sonnets from the Portuguese.*

Amarah is now twenty-four, and like her mama, she has a baby out of wedlock, though she and the father have been together for years. And Whoopi, who confided, "My face is sagging, my tits are on the side!" became a great-grandmother at fifty-six. She has two other grandchildren now, one of whom moved in and lived with her for a while. She tells me proudly, she has taught all the grandkids to cuss: "All the bad words. I'm like their playmate. They ask me, 'But have you always been like this?' and I'm like, 'Yeah, yeah. What are you gonna do?' and they're like, 'Okay!'" Like my friend Tish, she's discovering that grandmothering can be redemptive.

Another mother who handed off her child to the grandparents in order to follow her dreams was Stanley Ann Dunham, mother of the president of the United States. Barack Obama was raised by his white grandparents, Madelyn Dunham, whom he called "Toot," and Stanley Dunham, "Gramps." This was not a situation where they came over several days a week. When he was ten and living in Indonesia, his mother sent him off to live with Toot and Gramps in their apartment in Honolulu.

Before you even think about what kind of upbringing they provided, you have to wonder about a little boy's sense of abandonment, especially when his father had already left him. In Hawaii, however, the young Barack appears to have thrived. He did well at a fancy private prep school; he had the undivided attention of both a grandmother and a grandfather who adored him; and his mother did show up, from time to time.

Toot was said to be the one who brought stability and steadiness to her grandson's life. She was a career woman who had seen her share of sexism. After World War II, like Rosie the Riveter, she lost her job as an inspector for Boeing in Wichita when the men returned home from the front. Later, as a banker in Hawaii, she was tasked with training several men who would go on to become her bosses. She was of a time when "career paths" for women were cul-de-sacs.

Gramps was right out of *Death of a Salesman*, a defeated man who, ironically, may have given Obama his drive and ambition, though not in the way you might think. In his memoir, *Dreams from My Father*, Obama tells about hearing his grandfather's desperation as he was trying to sell insurance on the phone. "I could hear . . . Gramps's heavy sigh after he had hung up the phone, his hands fumbling through the files in his lap like those of a card-player who's deep in the hole." When still at prep school, young Barack wrote this poem for the literary magazine:

I saw an old, forgotten man
On an old, forgotten road.
Staggering and numb under the glare of the
Spotlight. His eyes, so dull and grey,
Slide from right to left, to right,
Looking for his life, misplaced in a
Shallow, muddy gutter long ago.
I am found, instead.
Seeking a hiding place, the night seals
    us together.
A transient spark lights his face, and in my hour,

He pulls out forgotten dignity from under his flaking coat,
And walks a straight line along the crooked world.

In his biography of Obama, David Maraniss speculates that it was Gramps's sense of failure that provoked Barack Obama into a productive life, since he never wanted to be where his grandfather ended up.

I once interviewed the president, for a *60 Minutes* piece in April 2009. We stood, as if I had just bumped into him roaming around the West Wing, only inches apart, much closer than if we were sitting knee to knee in a formal sit-down interview. What stood out, as it has for other journalists, was his repose, his inner calmness in the midst of the hubbub and tension in the White House. It felt almost aggressive. Can you thrust tranquility? I felt he did.

I thought about how even-keeled he was as president. Hardworking, a demonstrably devoted family man, he has the values that derive from a stable, nurturing upbringing. Grandparents who raise children cannot compensate for everything, but they can make up for a lot.

There are nearly three million grandparents in the United States who have legal custody of their grandchildren. A sizable share of them (18 percent) live below the poverty line. One of their many vexations is where to live. While there is subsidized housing for the elderly, children are usually not allowed. Overnight a grandmother might have to take in five kids, in which case she would be forced to move.

I learned about this problem in 2010, when I did a story with two of my favorite *60 Minutes* producers, Shari Finkelstein and Jennie Held, about a free after-school program in Harlem called Gospel for Teens. We started the shoot by going to auditions for that year's forty-six slots. The majority of the kids who tried out were African-American, living in rough neighborhoods.

At Gospel for Teens, the kids have to shout out their names and where they live. Rhonda Rodriguez was so withdrawn, she could barely whisper, and yet, because she sang "This Little Light of Mine" with riveting plaintiveness, she made the cut. And we decided to focus on her in our story.

Interviewing her hurt. At fourteen she exhaled dejection. In her forsaken little voice, she told us that she lived in the South Bronx in a very special building. When I asked why it was special, she said, "It's just for grandparents who are raising their grandchildren."

"Are you being raised by your grandparents?" I asked.

"I'm being raised by my great-grandmother." Her *great*-grandmother. That meant that neither her mother nor her father, nor any of her grandparents, had stepped in.

When we looked into the building, called the Grandparent Family Apartments, we learned it was constructed and funded by the city in 2004, in the heart of one of New York's lowest-income neighborhoods with one of the highest crime rates. When I went for a visit on a hot, steamy day in August 2014, I walked into a forest of tenements with exposed fire escapes, passing a playground where shirtless boys were playing basketball without a net and four old men were sitting in lawn chairs on the sidewalk in front of a Lucky 99 Cent Store. I thought I'd wandered into *The*

Wire. The clean, brightly painted six-story grandparents' building looked like someone who came to a party way overdressed.

I was buzzed in. The building has twenty-four-hour security—for good reason. Even with crime rates declining in New York City, this area still teems with drugs, and gunfire is an all-too-common punctuation mark of daily life. In February 2010, two of the children from the building were injured (not killed) in separate random street shootings.

Forty-five of the fifty apartments were headed by single grandmothers, or great-grandmothers. I was told it's the only building of its kind in the United States. Rhonda was living comfortably in a two-bedroom apartment with her great-grandmother Carmen Rivera, whom she calls Abuelita, "Grandma" in Spanish. When I met Carmen, she told me right up front: "I'm not the kind of grandmother that mopes around. Nope. I have a life. And I still raised my two kids, my two grandkids, and my two great-grandkids—so far."

What stood out was Carmen's sturdiness. She was wearing a blue fleece over tan slacks with white sneakers, no jewelry and no makeup. Except for her gray hair, you wouldn't have guessed she was seventy-one.

She'd been raising Rhonda since before she was one. Rhonda's mother had her at fifteen and started out taking care of her. But soon, said Carmen, "I saw things I didn't like. Before social services could intervene, I took it upon myself to go to court for custody." The judge told Carmen she would be eligible for roughly $11,000 a year if she took Rhonda as a foster child. But she said, "I didn't feel that was right." She forfeited the financial support but was rewarded when she was accepted into the building in 2005, the year it opened.

When I asked Carmen what it was like when Rhonda first came to her, she said, "It's hard in the beginning because you're accustomed to going to bed at a certain time, getting up at a certain time. You've raised your children and then you have to start all over again." She laughs. "Just to learn to put on Pampers! During my time there wasn't no Pampers."

"You were pinning cloth diapers the last time?"

She nodded. "And formula. It's all different. But there's help if you seek it. It's a sacrifice. But then it makes you feel good that you're capable of helping."

"I know my mother," Rhonda told me. "She comes around, like probably twice a year."

"What about your father?"

"I met him four or five years ago," she said.

"For the first time?"

"Yeah." I had to lean in to hear her. "He always promised me stuff and then, like, just broke his promises. One Halloween I waited for him for two or three, maybe four hours—just stood in the house. And then decided, 'Okay, I'll go trick-or-treating with one of my friends.'"

"That's painful," I managed to say.

"Yeah. But it's been happening all my life, so I'm pretty much used to it."

I reminded Carmen, "You told me that the kids here live with hurt inside."

"And nobody sees it but us."

Grandparents become guardians for a variety of reasons, none of them pretty. I met a young man in the Bronx building who had moved in with his grandmother after his mother died of leukemia. In other cases the parents are incarcerated or are drug addicts, or have mental illness, or have been accused of abuse. Or they simply leave.

The building offers the grans an array of services: legal assistance, transportation, mental health care, support groups and excursions, like one recently to a casino. Perhaps most important, there are parenting classes with lessons on how to talk about sex and drugs, and how to respond when a child says, "You're not my mother."

The building serves both the old and the young, so there are also after-school programs and tutors to help with homework. Report cards for all the children are sent to the office, where the grades are monitored. Seventy-four percent of the kids graduate from high school or obtain the GED. That compares with 49 percent in their school district and 59 percent in the Bronx as a whole.

"Most of our kids do really well," said the building manager Rimas Jasin, "though we've had one or two who've gone to jail, gotten pregnant or gotten hooked on drugs. But they're in a small minority."

To get into the building, a grandmother has to apply, so there is a self-selected population of motivated guardians, determined to "do it right this time." Jasin said, "There's a sense of having failed the first time. They see it as the least they can do, given the errors they made in the past. Whether they're actual errors or not, they blame themselves. Who's to know when your kid turns bad if it's your fault? But they're going to blame themselves anyway. That's part of the dynamic here."

There's a long waiting list to get into the building. To be eligible, a grandparent has to be at least sixty-two, with an average annual income of $18,000 or less, 30 percent of which they pay in rent. The residents are not what you might call a diverse population: 55 percent are African-American, 43 percent Hispanic. Only one grandmother is Caucasian.

One deficiency of the building is that it's a matriarchy. Not only are there few fathers in the children's lives, there are few grandfathers.

The afternoon I visited, six grannies in their seventies and eighties were playing bingo in one of the community rooms on the ground floor.

"Melvenia!" I said, seeing a familiar face. "How've you been?"

"Well, I'm just fine, except for this darn cane. My knees went out." I had first met Melvenia Smith ("A lotta folks jus' call me Miss Smith") three years before through a young girl named Yolanda Howard, another singer at Gospel for Teens. Yolanda is the youngest of three sisters Miss Smith has raised. But she's not their grandmother, she's their great-aunt.

"Why are you raising your grandnieces?" I asked.

"Their mother is mentally challenged and couldn't raise any of the three girls."

"What about their grandmother?"

"That's my sister. That's a totally different story that I will not get into."

At seventy-eight, Miss Smith is short, with mischievous eyes behind big round glasses. That day, she had red manicured nails, hair without a strand of gray, drop earrings and a stylish pantsuit. This is a woman who attends to her grooming.

She told me her grandparents may have been slaves in Alabama but said, "I have a paper that tells us they could read and write." She herself worked in a sweatshop until she moved from Alabama to New York in 1958 and became a bookkeeper for A&P, where she worked for twenty-three years while raising her five children. When I asked how many grandchildren she had, she had to think about it. Turns out she has seventeen, plus twenty-two great-grandchildren, and one great-great-grandkid.

When Yolanda was born, Miss Smith was sixty-one. She was already raising the new baby's two older sisters, Shakinah and Joslyn, and was determined not to add a third needy infant to the nest. "I had a full-time, fifty-hour-a-week job and two little kids.

"But then the older sister, Shakinah, says, 'You can't leave Yolanda in the hospital.' And I say, 'Yes I can.'" Miss Smith laughed, remembering. "'No no, Nanny, you gotta go get her.' And I say, 'No I don't. Nah, I'm not gonna get no baby. Y'all crazy. I'm gonna take care of no more babies. I'm too old.'" She laughed again, shaking her head.

"But I was there when she was born. See, this is the thing that really hooked me. I was there when she took her first breaths," she said. "God works in mysterious ways. The baby came out, the doctor wrapped her and put her in my hands. I'm lookin' down and she opened her eyes, looked at me, and started hollerin'. I was hooked like a fish. That was it."

Melvenia was a soul mate, another woman intoxicated by an infant. And it wasn't even her grandchild. "I just fell in love," she said, smiling. "Five days later she was mine." As with the older two, Melvenia went to court and won custody. "I got the first girl after three years, the middle one after three months, Yolanda after three seconds."

Listening to Melvenia reminded me of a heartbreaking story I did for *60 Minutes* in 2007 called "The Loneliest People on Earth," about the tens of thousands of American children who are taken away from their parents due to neglect or abuse. When a grandmother or another relative doesn't step in, most end up stranded in the child welfare system, shuttled in and out of foster homes. We found a few of them living in a treatment center in Los Angeles for troubled kids, many of them suicidal or engaged in self-destructive behaviors like cutting themselves. They were being helped by an organization called Family Finding. Its purpose: to search the country for a relative—an aunt, cousin, great-uncle—*any* relative who would take one of the kids home for Christmas or Thanksgiving. Psychologists say even that once-a-year connection would be like an elixir. So many of the kids had no one.

And here was a great-aunt who had plucked up three girls and redeemed them from what could have been a dreary, unconnected existence. Some of the grandmothers in the building see what they are doing as a sacrifice and an imposition; others see it as salvation. Miss Smith said raising grandchildren gives your life purpose. "I think I'm lucky. I think the girls are good for me because they stopped me from doin' a lot of things, like partying. I couldn't take care of them and have my social life at the same time, so I had to give that up."

"Well then, who saved who?" I asked.

"They saved me because at the rate I was going, partying every weekend, I might not be sitting here today."

Melvenia's baby Yolanda is strikingly beautiful, with a perfectly symmetrical face, arched eyebrows, and straight black hair in a pageboy. She gave me a paper she wrote about where they had lived before the Bronx: "There was no privacy there, not even enough room for doors, and when there was bad storms, the rats and pigeons would come in the house. Now I'm just loving where I live. It's clean."

She wrote matter-of-factly: "My mom, Priscilla, lives in Brooklyn in a home with people who have problems, but she loves me and I see her a lot. She had all three of us with three different men."

Her tone was free of self-pity and yet there was no disguising her pain. Even a grandmother's lavish affection cannot insulate these kids from the hurt of a parent's rejection. It's a festering wound. Miss Smith told me that Yolanda's father had come just once to see her. "He gave her twenty dollars and said, 'I'll be back on Sunday to take you to the movies.' He never showed up and that was a year ago. But at least, unlike her sisters, she knows who her dad is."

"I forgive him," Yolanda said, "because it wasn't his fault."

"Why wasn't it his fault?" I asked.

"Because he had to work. That was his excuse."

"But why do you say you forgive him? *I* don't forgive him. I don't. You're a child."

She looked at me with mournful eyes. "Yes."

"It's the fathers they break down over," said Miss Smith. "The girls think more about their fathers because we, as grandparents, we are women; we can take the mother's place, but we can't substitute for the father."

Yolanda may have yearned for her daddy, but she told me of the special bond she had with her great-aunt Melvenia: "I love her so much I don't know what I would do without her. She's my everything. I'm hers. I belong to her and her alone."

"Yolanda has anxieties," explained Miss Smith. "I know I'm the most important person in her life to be there, and I *am* there. Her biggest fear is who will take care of her if something happens to me. She comes home and if I'm not there and I don't answer my phone, there are twenty messages."

The downside for these children is the age of their grandparents. Fear of their dying pervades the building. So does the culture of the hood. The Bronx house is an attempt to end the cycle of abuse and the self-perpetuating society of unmarried mothers. But shiny and gleaming as the building is, it cannot entirely insulate its occupants from the meanness of its surroundings.

A year after my visit, I checked up on the girls from Gospel for Teens. Rhonda, who could barely whisper her name, finished high school. This was a triumph. But despite her upbringing in that secure enclave, she could not escape the pattern of her neighborhood. Rhonda had a baby out of wedlock at age seventeen and was pregnant again. Now that she has reached young adulthood (the grandchildren age out of the building in their late teens), her great-grandmother Carmen had to move out, though Rhonda is still living there with her baby. The staff is helping them find another place to live.

Yolanda is as close to her great-aunt, the stylish Miss Smith, as ever. She too graduated from high school and is now trying to develop a singing career.

But her oldest sister, Shakinah, twenty-three, is a single mom, and so is Joslyn, the middle sister, even though she went to college and graduate school, getting a master's degree in sociology. She moved back into the building with her one-year-old for a while. So Miss Smith, then a great-great-aunt, was sleeping on the couch in the living room. She said, "I live with stress—always."

It was Memorial Day weekend. Jordan was five months old, and Taylor and I sat on the couch in our New York living room, watching Jordan try to roll over, as if it were the best movie we'd ever gone to.

Taylor and Andrew went out the next night. That was the point of her coming home: to see friends, go to movies and plays, all the things new parents give up. Aaron and I consulted the precise instructions Tay had left with us. Item eight: Feed her at 9:30. By 9:10 Jordan was fidgety, so I warmed up her bottle of pumped milk and carried it and her to our bedroom, then, per item nine, we laid her down to sleep. But she squirmed and bawled and turned red. What about that sleep training? Clearly, it had stayed behind in Los Angeles.

I paced with her, bounced her, cradled and rocked her. Aaron tried. We swung her between us. Nothing we did settled her down. By 11:00 I was pretty agitated, having walked around the room the equivalent of five miles to the incessant sound of hair-curling wails. Trying my best to channel Taylor and stay calm, I wondered who the imbecile was who told me grandmothers tend to be more composed, more adaptive, not easily ruffled.

The meltdown held its force until Taylor got back and began breast-feeding. It took *me* thirty minutes to settle down, and then I lay awake fretting at my failure. If I had to do that every night, I would be done in. How on earth do those women in the Bronx do it? For most custodial grandparents, life can be hard physically, mentally and economically. There's no one for them to hand a kid over to in mid-tantrum.

New York City built the apartments to deal with two dramatic spikes in the number of grandparents gaining custody of their grandchildren. The first was in the early 1990s because of AIDS and the crack epidemic. The second was even steeper, in 2007–2008, brought on by the recession and the wars in Iraq and Afghanistan. The number of caretaker grandparents went up by 8 percent from 2000 to 2008. During the recession the largest increase was among whites, up 19 percent. There's a misconception that most custodial grandparents are African-American.

Little did I know when I started on this grandmother project that I had an expert on the subject right in the family. My sister-in-law, Paula, is a psychotherapist and educator in Boston who specializes in attachment disorders and foster care. She founded and runs Children's Charter Trauma Clinic for abused children and their families. When we spoke, her personal caseload included fifteen sets of custodial grandparents, most of them middle-class whites.

"I'm dealing with people raising young children by default," she says. "None of them chose to be a parent at this stage in their lives." Many of them got custody because their own son or daughter abused or neglected the children. So even before Paula deals with a child, she treats the grandparents. "In most cases," she said, "they're in mourning, first, over the ugly fact that their own child was an abuser, and second, that this isn't what life over sixty was supposed to be like." Many of them resent that their dream of a leisurely retirement was hijacked.

One of Paula's patients told her, "I'm sixty-four. I worked my whole life. I'm tired. I wanted something for *me*. Shit, it's not fair. I'm supposed to have the golden years. And now, again, there's nothing for me." So Paula has to deal with the grandparents' losses before anything else.

None of Paula's grandmothers live in an environment like the building in the Bronx, where there's security and services, and lessons in how to talk to adolescents. Most of her grandparents are on their own.

She told me about one of the couples she worked with—let's call them the Johnsons. He was a construction worker, she a waitress. "They were a frozen family. He was burning with rage at his daughter, going way back. He felt she was drinking and drugging just to make him miserable. And his anger only escalated when one day she just left her two-year-old on their doorstep. His wife took her cues from him, so there was not a single picture of the little girl's mother in her new house. I'm working with the ghost of their daughter," said Paula, "and this is pretty typical. I have to get through that wall."

With each case, Paula has to figure out what place in the family the biological parent should have. Can they visit? How often? Under what conditions? Some grandparents want a complete cutoff. Some of these mothers are in violent relationships. "The biological mother may have had her parental rights terminated by the courts," said Paula, "but she might be calling all the time, stalking, threatening: 'You took my kids away from me. It's your fault. I'll take care of you.' You would not believe what some of these grandparents go through."

One of the first things Paula did with the Johnsons was give them an assignment. "I gave them homework: to put up a photo of their daughter in the living room and give the little girl permission to talk about her mother." Then she gave them attachment exercises, showing Gramps how to blow cotton balls across the kitchen table and have the little girl blow them back. "You could see the grandfather transforming, laughing and giggling as if he was also five." And she had them dance together. Gramma too. "I had them hold her on their laps and gaze into her eyes."

"You're rewiring the little girl's brain," I said.

"No," said Paula, "I'm rewiring the grandparents' brains. Oxytocin"—that again—"was flooding their brains with love juice. It's the attachment fuel." Before long they adopted their grandchild.

In some of Paula's cases, she's dealing with a third generation of mistreatment. One of her single grandmothers was abused by her father; she went on to abuse her daughter, who abused *her* kids and then abandoned them. Paula is now trying to break the chain, that burden of inheritance. "These are people struggling not to do to their grandchildren what they did to their children." It hadn't occurred to me that handing an abused child over to their grandparents could thrust that child right back into an abusive environment.

Paula conceded that success with this group is "a mixed bag." These are people whose rage can go from zero to a hundred in a second. "I tell them when they get the urge to strike out, leave the room, breathe deeply, pick up a picture of the child when they were just a baby and gaze at it until they calm down. They're fighting an old alarm system that goes off. I tell them to rub their arms with ice cubes."

It's easier to reverse the damage done to the children "if [counselors] get the kids early," said Paula. "I believe the brain is plastic enough that a strong new attachment can make a huge difference in a child. Once they become adolescents it's pretty tough."

Even in a stable, loving home, when these children reach adolescence, they often exhibit emotional and behavioral problems. This is the age when they become more aware that their parents rejected them. Anger is a typical symptom, and who knows how many of these young people take it out on their aging grandparents.

And yet Paula tells stories about children who grow up in the direst of circumstances and still thrive later in life. The question is why some do and others don't. One possible reason is something known as the resiliency gene. Its real name is 5-HTT, and if someone has a certain mutation on it, he or she is likely to have, according to Emily Bazelon in the *New York Times*, "a buffer against the ruinous effects of adversity."

But even for those without the 5-HTT mutation, "a strong relationship with an adult who can be counted on daily, someone to talk to about personal problems, share good news with, get together with to have fun and seek advice . . . can mitigate the effects of abuse and produce a relatively successful life for a child." Enter Gramma.

Paula tells her grandmothers, "If you want to overcome the damage and create a healthy child, you need to provide a safe environment, and even more important, you need to signal that the child does not have to love you back. These kids don't believe anyone would love them. You have to show them you do, and that you do without expecting anything in return." A good lesson for any grandparent.

I told her about Rhonda, Shakinah and Joslyn, the young unmarried mothers in the Bronx, and asked if their grans had failed. Paula wondered if being a single mom was even a measure of "failure" anymore. We know that lots of unmarried women who do not grow up in the poorest pockets of the country are having babies. And new polls show that approval of unwed parenthood has risen dramatically from 45 percent in 2001 to 61 percent today.

"So, what should I say about the girls?" I asked.

"You have to see how these young woman are as parents," said Paula. "If they can provide their own children essential love and attachment that they internalized from their grandmothers, then it's a success." The cycle of deprivation of love will have been broken. And that is not an insignificant accomplishment.

"One more thing," said Paula. "Grandparents who raise their grandchildren are too often an anonymous part of our society. They are brave and selfless and rarely get support from their communities. To me," she said, "they're unsung heroes."

FIVE

Working Grannies

The idea that no one is perfect is a view most commonly held by people with no grandchildren.

—DOUG LARSON

In colonial America life expectancy was short, so there weren't that many grandmothers. But those women who did survive into old age were like early grandmas: they watched over the toddlers so both parents could work their farms and have more babies.

With the transition to a more urban and industrialized economy in the early 1900s, the elderly came to be seen as more of a burden. But then along came Social Security and Medicare. Together they allowed grandparents to live independently.

We're now entering another new phase where more and more of us gray-heads are refusing to leave our jobs just as young adults are delaying getting theirs. It's as though there's some biological imperative at work. While our generation left home and launched our careers at twenty-one, today our children are waiting till they're thirty-one. We're all postponing growing up or, in our case, growing old. All the passages are lengthening. The millennials, aged twenty to thirty-five, our grandchildren, are still living at home—roughly a quarter of them. So many, it's become acceptable. The dating site Match.com even offers tips on how to conduct a social and sex life under the heading "Dating at Mom and Dad's House."

At the same time, by putting off retirement and continuing to earn, we older Americans are extending our independence. This means that many of us are able to send money for our grandchildren's education, medical bills and day care. As a generation we're deeply embedded in their lives.

My continuing to work at *60 Minutes* has little to do with contributing to Jordan's well-being (though I do). I work because it's healthy (for me) physically and mentally. My mother always used to say, "A busy mind is a happy mind." And it's a good thing for Jordan to have a working mother whose sense of self is not a corollary of her child's success. Even though working moms (I'm guessing 99.9 percent of them) walk around with a misery of self-reproach, there's something reassuring that happens when we send the kids off to day care or into the arms of a nanny. Our babies always know we're their moms. They just know.

I was helped in the guilt department by a wonderful gift Dolly gave me: permission, in fact an order, to go back to work after Taylor was born. So many of my friends' mothers used to ladle out the accusations: "How *could you* leave little Johnny? What's wrong with you?" Dolly agreed with Taylor's pediatrician, who told me that the secret to good parenting is a happy mother. For some of us, keeping our jobs is the road to our child's mental health. I always knew Taylor was better off with me expending my energy at the office than me hovering over her until she hated me.

Naturally there were regrets over all the things I missed. They piled up. Once CBS assigned me to cover the White House in 1979, I lost control of my schedule. A White House correspondent is always on what they call "body watch." We have to be where the president is, so if he travels, we travel, even if it's on short notice. When Prime Minister Ohira of Japan died in 1980, Jimmy Carter decided to go to Tokyo for the funeral on that very day, which meant my getting on the press plane instead of seeing Taylor in a school play. That was my life from the time she was two until she was fourteen.

While I was able to catch the occasional soccer match, and once saw her play right tackle on her school's junior varsity football team (that was something to behold: my little angel grunting in the mud), I was basically, and I say this ruefully, AWOL for most of her athletic career.

As long as I'm confessing, the most shameful thing I missed was Taylor's being rushed to the hospital when she was ten, complaining of severe stomach cramps. Dr. Ross, the pediatrician, thought it was appendicitis. I was stuck in the White House press room, unable to leave because the "lid" was off, meaning President Carter was in the Oval Office.

Aaron kept calling from the hospital with bulletins: we're in the emergency room, waiting; she's being examined; they just took her off for an ultrasound. I was nauseous with fear and frozen with indecision. Shouldn't I just leave? What kind of a mother was I? Just as I was about to desert my post, Aaron called again: "She has the flu. We're going home."

Reporting from the lawn of the White House, May 23, 1980.

Another encroachment on my time—ensuring that I was a walking stress factory—was *Face the Nation*, which I moderated on Sunday mornings from 1983 to 1991. (Our motto was: "Watch us *before* you go to church, so you'll know what to pray for!") But more to the point, I also worked part of the weekend. I must have been insane.

I didn't miss Taylor's entire childhood. When I traveled, I took her with me whenever I could. Once we went home with Jimmy Carter to Plains, Georgia, a small town nasty with gnats. We stayed at the Best Western in nearby Americus, where somehow Taylor, at age one, fell into the swimming pool. Without worrying about my hair (there haven't been many minutes of that in my entire career!), I jumped in after her.

When the Reagans went to their ranch in the Santa Ynez Mountains, Taylor stayed with me at the press hotel in Santa Barbara. I threw her fourth-birthday party on the beach with a cake, a clown and Sam Donaldson (and the rest of the White House press corps). We were combatants during the day, pals after deadline.

As she grew up I took Taylor shopping and helped with homework whenever I could, though I'm embarrassed to say we would often study for her tests or work on her papers over dinner in restaurants. And I went to teacher conferences, which didn't always go well, like the time I asked Tay's favorite eighth-grade English teacher when her baby was due. Oops. That protuberance wasn't what I thought it was. My anxiety attacks over that one lasted for weeks.

One day when George H. W. Bush was president, the First Lady invited a small group of reporters to lunch upstairs in the residence. We got onto the subject of parenting, and Mrs. Bush held forth on working moms, warning that no matter how tired we are at the end of the day, how grumpy, how sore at our boss, when we go home, we'd better stifle all that and walk in the door as if it's first thing in the morning, and give our children our fresh, happy-I'm-with-you attention. The subtext: otherwise

At the White House Easter Egg Roll with Taylor, 1981.

you're a rotten mother. This hit me hard. If anybody needed that lecture, it was me.

After lunch, Mrs. Bush gave us a tour of the living quarters. I had to smile when we got to the Lincoln Bedroom because it looked like my bedroom, with toys all over the place. The Bushes loved having their grandchildren stay over.

I recently asked Taylor about our years in Washington. "How much *did* I miss? And how much did you resent it?" I have no memory of her ever complaining.

"I don't remember your absence as much as I remember Dad always being there," she said. "He was the at-home parent. With him there, I never felt abandoned."

Aaron threw himself into parenting with relish. He was a chaperone on all her school field trips, including camping out. He sat with Tay while she learned to read and work out arithmetic problems, helped her build her science projects and write her history and English papers. Aaron read (or reread) every single book she was assigned from first grade through graduation—from college.

"I remember going to my friends' houses," said Taylor, "and thinking: This is so annoying having so-and-so's mom lurking around. If I had friends over, Dad was there"—his office was in the apartment—"but he left us alone."

He was an exceptionally obliging father. When she wanted to learn to scuba dive, he took the classes with her. They certified together and would go off every once in a while on father-daughter diving trips.

My main role was scheduler-in-chief. I tried keeping Taylor's days full, booking her for ballet, piano lessons, gymnastics, tap

Aaron and Taylor while he worked on Urban Cowboy *in 1979.*

dancing and art classes. That way, I figured, maybe she wouldn't notice I wasn't there. I made the playdates and the doctor appointments. Someone asked me back then what I liked to do in my leisure time. What were my hobbies? Was she serious? My pastime was holding things together, which is how I developed CCLD, Chronic Compulsive List Disorder.

"How did you do it—have a demanding job and raise a kid?" I

hate that question. But forced to answer, I'd say: my mother said go for it, my husband was a talented father, and we were able to afford a full-time nanny at no insignificant expense. The cost of day care eats up a major chunk of a working mother's income. Increasingly, grandparents are stepping in to pay for some or all of the costs.

I asked economist Betsey Stevenson of President Obama's Council of Economic Advisers about the struggles of working moms. She's an expert on the economics of everyday life. Over lunch at the Washington Marriott she told me that she and her partner, Justin Wolfers—like her, a Harvard PhD economist—put together a flowchart of the most sensible way to spend their money when their daughter, Mathilda, was born. They wanted to carve out undivided time to spend with her and hold on to their busy careers.

What their analysis showed was that they should devote a sizable portion of both their incomes to a five-star nanny, so they could go to work with peace of mind. After sifting through statistics and pie charts, they concluded that the best pool of potential nannies for their daughter was young schoolteachers. They found someone with a master's degree in education and lured her with a salary of $50,000 a year, far more than she was likely to earn in any classroom. They also hired someone to drive them to their jobs so they could work in the car. Together this was a big bite out of their combined salaries. Obviously it's a solution very few can afford, though given their pooled income, it's somewhat proportional to what most middle-class two-income families are spending, depending on where they live. The average cost of full-time day care varies across the country. In New York it's $14,500 a year; in California, $11,628; in Alabama, $5,547. In most states high-quality child care is more expensive than college.

While Betsey Stevenson shares the family's bread-and-butter decision-making with her partner, more and more it's women who solely control the family purse strings. At some point in their lives, 95 percent of American women will be responsible for their family's finances, and many of them are grandmothers. We've seen a seismic gender shift when it comes to money, as women inherit, earn and control over $3 trillion in the United States.

Just when I thought I was getting my personal-professional juggling act under control in Washington, Mike Wallace of *60 Minutes* called and asked me if I wanted to come join him and work at the most-watched news program in America. Of course I wanted to. Who wouldn't? But there were downsides. I would have to move to New York, then the murder, homeless, squeegee and litter capital of the country. More troubling was the prospect of uprooting Taylor, then fourteen, from her school in Washington to bring her to this dystopia of a city, where she didn't have a single friend. When I decided to take the plunge and told her the news, my little girl didn't stop crying until I agreed she didn't have to take piano lessons anymore.

No longer tied to the president's schedule, I hoped I'd have more control of my time and be able to organize my life around Taylor's activities. And for the really big events, I could. But I had to travel more than ever. When Don Hewitt, the legendary executive producer of *60 Minutes*, hired me, he warned me I'd be on the road most of the time. He wasn't exaggerating. In that first year, I went to eighteen different cities in nine countries, from Romania and Iraq to Israel and Russia. Was I ever home? No. And yes, I suffered. What kind of a mother was I?

As in Washington, Aaron was the primary parent, but now he did *all* the homework with Taylor, and there was a lot. At least I was home on the weekends. Saturdays and Sundays were Taylor's, if she wanted to be with her mother. That's the thing: just as I was freer, she was busier with her friends.

Moving to a new school turned out to be a boon for Tay since she got to reinvent herself. And she became more independent. It had bothered me that in Washington she had to be driven everywhere, constantly under the supervision of adults. Now at last she was on her own, taking the bus to school and the subway down to Greenwich Village, or wherever else she wanted to explore.

She and I were both acclimating to new surroundings and new routines. I had been warned that *60 Minutes* was a testosterone locker room, but everyone was welcoming—Mike; Morley; Ed Bradley; Steve Kroft; Don, the boss; and Andy Rooney. Outside of a little elbowing—Mike picked off my interview with Barbra Streisand—I felt comfortable as one of the guys.

The only sour note came a month or so after I started. I was interviewed for a documentary about *60 Minutes*. The first question was something like: "You must be in awe working with all these giants. What's it like for you to be up here in the pantheon?"

I felt they were patronizing me. Weren't they suggesting I wasn't "a giant," and should be in awe? I was always determined not to cry sexism. If I had a setback, it was my fault: I had to work harder. But this time, it boiled over. Silly me. I thought I had earned the job, that I belonged at *60 Minutes*. It seemed to me that my credentials (chief White House correspondent, ten years; moderator of *Face the Nation*, eight years; coanchor with Charles Kuralt of *America Tonight*, two years) were enough to admit me to the club as an equal. But all the documentarians saw was "the girl." I seethed inside.

I said nothing, though, ducking the question. It bothered me for days but then melted away because I had just landed the best job in broadcast journalism. I loved what I was doing. I smiled so much that first year, my face hurt.

Each of the correspondents has his or her own team of producers. Most on my team were in their thirties, married with children. I told them that as far as I was concerned, their kids came first. I was stunned one day when producer Cathy Olian confessed that she was terrified to take time off if one of her kids was sick.

"But I told you I would understand," I said.

"I know, but I'm still afraid you'll think I'm not reliable or as available as one of the men."

I thought that fear—that tending to our children would lead to penalties, which I had felt so acutely thirty-five years before—had been snuffed out long ago. It was perplexing that it was still there, even with a female boss who truly was sympathetic.

Boy, was I naïve. For tens of millions of low-wage women in America, taking time off from work because a child has a sore throat, or because school closes unexpectedly for a snow day, puts their jobs at risk. They could be and are being fired.

The lucky ones have a grandma they can call on in such emergencies.

The dreaded day came when our only child went off to college. I cried all the way back from dropping Taylor off. But by the end of that first week, I had a big surprise. I realized that I had been living in a permanent state of aggravated anxiety. From the day Taylor was born, I had walked around with an insidious gnawing that I would forget a doctor's appointment or leave her stranded somewhere. What if she was sick or in an accident and I couldn't get to her? I had nightmares that she would turn to drugs or get her heart broken. Would the girls be mean to her? Would she get acne? As she got older, when she was out at night, I would sit up hugging my knees till she got home.

But within days of her going to college, the weight of all that lifted. Just like that. I wasn't sure why—she was still my baby, I still spoke to her every day and I still worried about her. But that ever-present foreboding was gone, along with the pangs of conscience. I could travel, work late, sleep all day Sunday. I always told Tay I was miserable without her, and I was. But there is that dirty little secret about the empty nest: we moms get our freedom back, and it's heady.

My daughter loved college, where she double-majored in English and geology (the only science with a story line) and spent her winter weekends on the ski team. The minute she graduated, she moved to LA to pursue a dream she'd had ever since Aaron took her to the set of *Perfect*, a film he wrote in 1984. She wanted to make movies.

Within a short time, she was working at a movie production company called Middle Fork, which is where she met Andrew and fell in love.

More than half of all American grandmothers are not yet senior citizens. They're still working age. But as they cross that line, more and more, like me, they're kicking retirement down the road. So by continuing to work into my seventies, I'm part of a trend. Up to 60 percent of sixty-five-year-olds are putting off retirement, and a third of sixty-eight-year-olds. You could say working grandparents are a brood of spring chickens, afraid if they retire they'll be bored or feel they were benched. Working keeps them feeling young, the boomer Holy Grail. I assume that all the above applies to the septuagenarian rockers who won't give it up. I'm talking about you, Mick, and you, Keith, still blasting our eardrums out on tour—in your torn jeans and ponytails. The *New York Times* said, "The rock 'n' roll dinosaurs . . . are not going quietly into the pop culture twilight." Same for all the action-hero sexagenarians like Bruce Willis, Harrison Ford and I'll-be-back Arnold, still jumping off tall buildings and crushing the bad guys.

Another reason so many grandparents stay on the job is simply because they need the money and health benefits. It used to be that you'd retire, and if you were in good shape, you'd live another ten years. All your retirement plans were built on that assumption and another one: that if necessary your grown children would take care of you. But grandparents are realizing they can no longer rely on either. For one thing, they're going to live a lot longer, most of us for another twenty to thirty years. What was once enough to retire on doesn't come close anymore.

The other catch is that as a group, grandparents are wealthier than their children. Most sixty- and seventy-year-olds have more money than forty- and fifty-year-olds, which is something we haven't seen before. So who's going to take care of whom? The mean household income of boomer grandparents is about $80,000, while their offspring's is 9 percent lower. We're spring chickens and rare birds!

Consider this: If you retire at sixty-two, your Social Security benefit will be less than $12,000 a year; wait until you're seventy, and it jumps to $35,000. It almost triples. No wonder so many keep working, especially when they're spending more than they ever planned to caring for their own aging parents (more and more of whom are living into their nineties) and at the same time helping support their children and grandchildren.

According to a Gallup poll, 70 percent of US workers hate their job. But that leaves 30 percent who don't. That could be because about a third of the baby boomers are college graduates who became professionals and white-collar workers. Unlike their dads, with their mechanical or arduous lift-and-lug jobs, they actually like what they do. Many of them, like me, stay in the game because they don't want to stop doing what they love.

The hitch to grandparents' working is that they don't get to see their grandchildren enough. We're continuing to contend with the same old work-life balance issues. Alice Greenwald, the director of the 9/11 Memorial Museum at Ground Zero, has had an all-consuming job creating and curating the museum, and dealing with the sensitivities of the victims' families. "It's been late nights and weekends," she tells me.

Like the rest of us, she can't get enough of her grandson, Ezra, but her job keeps impinging. "Even though I live nearby, I'm not available to babysit as much as I or they would like. I try to see the baby every weekend, so I'm always having to clutch for time for me. He's my number one priority. If it's him versus me, he wins every time."

When Alice's daughter had Ezra, she stopped working and decided to use cloth diapers.

"Really?" I say, thinking how lucky I was Taylor didn't do that.

"Yup," she says, with a raised eyebrow. "Those diaper pins are hard. Plus, I'm out of practice on everything else. It's been twenty-eight years."

We talk about how our daughters have so few ways to rebel. We like the same music, same clothes, same haircuts. The only thing left is child-rearing. Therefore all the new rules, like the importance of "tummy time," and the once-obsolete practices of using diaper pins and glass bottles. It's getting so difficult to keep up (or go back) that some grans are going to grandparent classes to learn about the dos and don'ts and the latest gadgets, like the snot-sucker and diapers with moisture sensors that beep when the baby pees.

As an aside, Alice told me that before her recent job, she ran the Holocaust Memorial Museum in Washington, DC, where she learned that most survivors of the concentration camps never talked to their children about what had happened to them. But they tell their grandchildren. They said in video interviews that they didn't want to burden their own kids with their pain. But they tell their grandchildren because they want the story to be passed on to the next generation.

Like Alice, I'm always trying to squeeze in time to be with Jordan. I'm lucky in that at *60 Minutes*, everyone takes the month of July off. When Jordan was six months old in the summer of 2011, Aaron and I rented a house in Santa Barbara, a California-style ranch with a lush flower garden, and lured Taylor and Andrew to come stay with us.

I got to play with Jordan every day for four weeks. She chewed on my fingers, grabbed for my earrings, my glasses, my necklace. She put her fingers in my mouth and loved when I'd draw on them as if they were straws. I held her on my lap, smelling her baby perfume—Jordan extract.

But after an hour or so of this, to be perfectly honest, I found myself praying she'd fall asleep. And this was a baby I adored. Entertaining an infant who can't talk is hard work. Though I had far more patience with Jordan than I ever did when Taylor was an infant.

One day when I'd finally rocked Jordan to sleep, I turned on the TV. There was Rupert Murdoch and his son James being grilled by a parliamentary committee in London about their newspapers' phone hacking. I had to smile. Only a few months earlier I had interviewed Murdoch Sr. before an audience at a school benefit. I asked him if he agreed with Warren Buffett that billionaires like both of them should pay more in taxes. I was surprised when Rupert said, "Yes, I agree." There was a pause, then he added: "I agree with Warren—that *he* should pay more in taxes!" It got a big guffaw.

When Jordan got fussy, Aaron would rock her. It was the best scene ever: little baby girl asleep in big Aaron's arms. Taylor called him the baby whisperer. At other times, Andrew would get down on the rug with Jordan and pretend to eat her tummy like a noisy wolf. Her funny daddy was wild with love. Tay says, "Andrew entertains, I comfort."

And every couple of days Tay would bind Jordan to her chest in an Ergobaby wrap, and off we'd go to one of the Santa Barbara beaches, where we would unleash their dog, Sydney. She'd scamper onto the sand and chase tennis balls into the surf. The waves hit the beach, children played, dogs splashed, I got to hold my granddaughter, and I thought: Ain't life grand.

Back at work in New York, producer Rich Bonin, video editor Richard Buddenhagen, and I were screening an interview with the prison warden at Guantánamo Bay. It was part of an important story, one we would win an Emmy for. At the time we were struggling to get it right, and to cut out three minutes, disagreeing about which parts of the Q-and-A we could and couldn't live without. It was the usual: we started out listening politely to each other's suggestions, but soon the courtesies gave way, and the shouting began. "Are you nuts? That's the best thing he says." We were concentrating, agonizing, forgetting how much fun our jobs were. And then my cell phone pinged. I couldn't ignore it. It was

Taylor. She had sent me a video of Jordan at a park chasing after a little boy. The tension in my neck eased and the lines between my eyebrows unpinched as I chuckled and passed it around. It took a while to recover my focus. Ten minutes later Bonin's phone rang. It was his daughter Abbey. She'd gotten an A on her test. In another five minutes Richard got an e-mail from his son in college. A typical day at *60 Minutes*.

Rich Bonin and I have worked together for twenty years. He's a meticulously thorough researcher and investigator, which is not a surprise, since he was trained by Mike Wallace. One of his gifts is using his considerable charm to persuade the most reluctant general, CEO or prison warden to give us an interview. And believe me, there aren't many generals, CEOs or prison wardens begging to be on our broadcast.

When Rich got divorced he won joint custody of his two daughters, Abbey and Olivia. He struggled with how he was going to raise them and continue to travel three or four months of the year. No question he needed help. Then the idea came to him: he would ask his widowed mother, who lived in California, to come east and move in with them. "She said yes for two reasons," he told me. "One, she's an Italian mother, meaning she lives for her children, and two, because all her friends were dying and she was spending her days in front of her TV, just waiting for the sun to go down."

So there he was, a *mammone*—a hard-bitten journalist in his forties living with his mother. Who became a granny nanny. He used to tell me there was no one who loved his children more, and no one he trusted more.

Being a grandmother was my new identity. And I was fast becoming a stereotype. Whenever I passed a store that sold anything for babies, man, was I sucked in. Dresses, little shoes, toys, books. If you came to our apartment in New York right now, you'd see a dollhouse in the hallway, a little stove by the kitchen, a miniature baby grand piano in the living room, a huge stuffed dog, a baby rocking chair. You can walk into any room and know we're grandparents.

I am so not alone. Grandparent spending on child-specific items has increased sevenfold in the last ten years. We're out there buying baby food, equipment, clothing, tricycles and toys. Our grandchildren melt our wallets! One day I took Jordan to buy some books at Barnes and Noble. One of the few bright spots in their world of Amazon competition is children's books, which continue to sell briskly in hardcover. B&N helps this along by selling toys, often on display amid the books. So there I was with Jordan flipping through *Angelina Ballerina* when she spotted the dolls. "Okay," I said, "but just one." I ended up buying three, one of which cost $60. I am convinced there's a gramma gene that disables the word "no."

Beyond buying them stuff, grandparents are helping their children with mortgage payments, day care and divorce attorneys. We can—and do—pay for our grandkids' medical and orthodontist bills and school tuition. These expenses are not treated as gifts by the IRS as long as you make the payments directly to the school or doctor. As a group, grandparents spend roughly $2.5 billion a year on primary and secondary school tuition.

Grans can also invest in a 529 plan for college and postgraduate expenses, and if they can afford it, each grandparent can make tax-free gifts each year of up to $14,000 to each one of their grandchildren, their children and their children's spouses.

Many grandparents struggle to help support their grandchildren, and others do it grudgingly, feeling their kids are taking advantage of them or shirking their responsibilities, knowing the grandparents will serve as "the emergency bank." But whether happily or reluctantly, grandparents are contributing. Pinchas Cohen, dean of the USC Davis School of Gerontology, says there are three stages of life. In the first stage, you believe in Santa Claus; in the second you don't believe in Santa Claus; and in the third, you *are* Santa Claus!

Being a working mother means toggling between both seats of a seesaw, always compensating for the weight of work on one side and the responsibility of a child on the other. It takes constant managing, straddling, offsetting. As a working grandmother you have to deal with the same search for the balance-of-life sweet spot you did as a mother. If you live across the country, that means becoming a magician. You have to either be in two places at the same time or turn them into one place, which is what I did by urging my team at *60 Minutes* to find as many stories for me as possible in Southern California. So the hunt was on.

Producer Shachar Bar-On found one in the fall of 2011 in Riverside, an hour east of LA. Shachar has been on the team ever since we heard about the best news producer at NBC News and lured him away in 2006. He's Israeli born and raised, and a father of two boys I love, Jonathan, now twelve, and Benami, eight. Shachar has invited me to two events I had never attended before: his swearing-in ceremony when he became a US citizen, and Benami's bris.

The story he found involved a grandmother, Joann Patterson, whose son, Jeff Hall, the leader of a *Sieg heil*–ing neo-Nazi group, was murdered in 2011. He was killed in his living room by his own son, ten-year-old Joe.

Shachar and I had assumed the murder had something to do with all the gun-toting and hate-filled fascist ranting around the Hall household. But the more we dug, the less that seemed a factor. For most of his life little Joe had been a volatile and violent child who had been kicked out of six schools, including one for disturbed children.

About Joe's shooting his dad, his grandmother Joann said, "I wasn't surprised by it. I just somehow felt it could always happen." She was an attractive, sixty-something high school biology teacher, trim with straight auburn hair. The day I interviewed her she was so composed as she told me the gruesome details, I thought she must be on a sedative.

"There aren't too many good days. It's a struggle every minute of my life." While her delivery was unemotional, the horror of what had happened still came through: her beloved son was shot at point-blank range by her beloved grandson.

This is the hardest part of my job. Not asking officials a tough question about policy or their behavior. Not holding a business executive to account. It's eliciting heartbreaking testimony from grieving parents or grandparents.

I ached for Joann as she described her push-me, pull-you feelings for young Joe. "When he killed my son," she said, "I hated him. I really wrestle with it because my son was murdered and I want justice for him. But that only happens at the expense of my grandson." Her eyes were pools of pain. "I go visit Joe once a week. There are times when I just can't look at him." She looked down. "There's always a guard with us. So I mean, it's not like there's any danger." She let out a terrible, grim laugh.

Joann wanted Joe sent to a psychiatric facility, but he was sentenced to ten years of juvenile detention, with the possibility of parole in seven. He'll be set free by the time he's twenty.

When I said good-bye, I thought: If I ever live through a tragedy, I want what she's on.

I jumped in a car as soon as I could and sped to LA. Or tried to. I could've walked faster than the traffic moved on the 91 freeway. I just stared out the window, unable to shake Joann's heavy gloom.

When I got to Taylor and Andrew's, Jordan was in a high chair, Tay "zoom zoom"–ing freshly pureed spinach into her mouth. When the food went in, Jordan put her fist in after, thus decorating her pink dress with lumpy green flecks. I wanted to devour the whole package.

"Yaw-yi," she said—that's "Lolly"—her legs pumping with I-love-you eagerness. I mopped up the dinner debris and her teething drool, picked her up and brought her into the living room, now her playroom. Jordan's favorite thing was to stand at her activity table, a plastic contraption that honked, rang, buzzed and counted in English and Spanish as she pushed knobs and twirled a dial that turned on songs like "Old MacDonald Had a Farm."

One round of e-i-e-i-o with Jordan and my sadness from interviewing Joann Patterson was gone.

California was so rich with stories, I practically shuttled to LA in Jordan's first two years of life. I know that traveling across the country several times a year is something most people can't afford. As it does with so many facets of life today, income inequality has a bearing on how we grandparent. It's one of the reasons more and more grans are selling their homes after they retire and moving near the grandkids.

One of the more memorable interviews I did in LA in that period was with bodybuilder, movie star, former governor Arnold Schwarzenegger. My first impressions of him: he was shorter than I had thought, and he was great fun to be with. After several days of following him around, I sat opposite him in his office and quizzed him about his affair with his housekeeper, Mildred, their illegitimate son and the consequent breakup of his marriage with Maria Shriver. Usually when I ask embarrassing personal questions, I get nervous and my insides knot up, but for some reason, not that day, as I asked how he found out that Mildred's son was his.

"He started looking like me," said Arnold, steady and clear-eyed. In fact, he answered all my questions without complaint, no matter how invasive or accusatory, like one about his wife: "She gave up her television career for you," I scolded. "Wow. Was this just the most unbelievable act of betrayal to Maria?"

"It was terrible," he said, looking right into my eyes. "I inflicted tremendous pain on Maria and unbelievable pain on the kids . . . This is something that I will always look back on and say, 'How could you have done that?'"

I had the feeling Arnold wanted me to ask the toughest questions we could come up with so he could get a spanking on national television. It would be his mea culpa and, he hoped, an expiation.

There's a reason Mike Wallace hung on at *60 Minutes* deep into his grandfather years. Same for Morley and Andy Rooney (who was a great-grandfather). Every story we do is an education, a chance to make a difference and an opportunity to meet the most accomplished people in a given field. I've interviewed Peter Higgs of the Higgs boson, Mark Zuckerberg (twice) of Facebook and Steven Spielberg, to name three.

But it's not just the marquee names. I get to know people in so-called ordinary life who are extraordinary. Emergency room doctors, farmers contending with drought, inner-city schoolteachers, tunnel diggers.

But mainly I keep working because it's fun, the work itself. I come across women like me all the time, grandmothers who keep at it because they take pride in what they do and feel they're helping others. As long as you're healthy, it's hard to give up what gives you pleasure and purpose.

Something else in my case is that at *60 Minutes* we usually find our own stories, which means I'm committed to and interested in every one. And because we spend weeks on them, bringing them to life, nurturing them, I come to see each story as my child. Or nowadays, my grandchild.

One such report—in California—was "The Oldest Old," about people living long lives, free of dementia. It was produced by Shari Finkelstein (my partner in the Gospel for Teens piece that led me to the grandparents' building in the Bronx). Shari has preteen twin girls who are brilliant, adorable and nice. I, like everyone else, want to know how she does it all. Like so many other working moms, her answer is, "I don't know."

One of the many things I love about Shari is her offbeat enthusiasms. For instance, she loves zydeco, which is Cajun music played with accordions and washboards. She has been known to travel great distances just to hear a zydeco band. (Factoid: Aaron wrote a play called *Pogo and Evie*, the one and only zydeco musical, which was performed at the New York International Fringe Festival in 2007.)

Anyway, Shari thinks on the bias. When you see one of her pieces you're inclined to say, "Only *60 Minutes* would do a story like that," or "Gee, I didn't know that!" which Don Hewitt used to tell us was our gold standard.

"The Oldest Old" was about a massive research study of people over ninety in Irvine, south of LA. We all say we dread becoming really old, because we assume we'll be frail and infirm. But a surprising number of people over ninety today aren't feeble at all. The over-ninety crowd is the fastest-growing segment of the US population, and a large percentage is doing remarkably well. Shari had me interview eight people in the study from age ninety-three to one hundred, most of them as strong and quick-witted as sixty-year-olds, and several as into sex as thirty-year-olds.

Some of what the study determined is pretty obvious, like exercise extends life, and it doesn't have to be strenuous. Walking at an easy pace for fifteen to forty-five minutes a day adds years.

But other findings were surprising, if not thrilling. For instance, alcohol in moderation is good for you. It seems that people who drink up to two glasses a day have a 15 percent reduced risk of death, compared to nondrinkers. And it's not just wine. It's any of the spirits. Coffee's also good for you. And, a shock to me—and all those Washington lobbyists hired by the health supplement industry—vitamins don't seem to contribute much of anything to one's healthiness.

My favorite discovery was that by ninety, it's best to be *overweight,* with *high* cholesterol. Bottom line: if we grandparents live that long, we can enjoy a highball every night and share those fudge brownies we've been depriving ourselves of all these years—with our grandbabies.

Each of the stories shot in California either started or ended with a trip to see Jordie. Taylor was a late bloomer. She walked late, talked late and read late. When I used to open T. Berry Brazelton each month for a development check, I was a wreck. Jordan was the opposite. By her first birthday, she had the vocabulary of an average two-year-old. "Apple." "Up." "Puppy." "Tor-tu" (turtle). When she said "La La," I declared, "That's Lolly!" She could also sign. Andrew gave me a list of words she could "say" with her hands: "bean," "thank you," "cookie," "mouse." One hundred four in all.

She was still kind of bald, though wisps of hair the color of a palomino were coming in. Her eyes were a vivid blue. I couldn't stop staring at her. She was, without question, ravishing. On one visit I took my little genius to Toddle Tunes for a music lesson with fifteen other one-year-olds. We hit tambourines, plucked a mandolin, sang and clapped. All delightful until Jordan began grabbing maracas away from the other children. "We have to share, Jordan," I said, but without the strain in my voice I had had with Taylor when *she* was grabbing toys from the other kids.

Afterward, I took Jordan to a park. This had been my least-favorite thing to do with Taylor. Yet there I was, happily pushing Jordan on a swing. "More, La La," she said between bursts of infectious, merry laughter. I was wearing a hat and dark glasses, slinking around, praying I wouldn't be recognized. I wanted to shut out everything but her.

That night Taylor, Andrew, Jordan and I went out to a nice restaurant. I thought my angel face might be having early-onset terrible twos. The only way to keep her from disrupting everyone else's dinner with piercing shrieks was to let her watch *Winnie the Pooh* on Tay's iPad. She called him "Pee Boo."

It's embarrassing when a one-year-old is more fluent in a language (albeit Web-speak) than you are. She was, even at that age, in danger of being addicted to the iPad. Like most young parents today, Tay and Andrew were trying to keep Jordan away from all electronic devices for that very reason. They succumbed only in restaurants and on airplanes, but even those little doses are enough to hook a kid.

I met a woman who told me: "I'm not Gramma Ice Cream Cone or Gramma Candy, I'm Gramma iPad." Me too. Mommy says, "No." We say, "Sure. Anything you want." I acknowledge this shamefacedly, that I introduced Jordan to the most fun app, called Cookie Doodle, where you mix, bake and decorate every kind of cookie you've ever heard of. I showed Jordan how to sift flour, break eggs, add in sugar and stir on an iPad. "Again, La La, again." We made 143 batches. Tay accused me of being a drug dealer.

On one of my trips to California, as I was racing to be with Jordan, I thought about what it means to grow up. I decided it means that you watch time flow backward. First, when you raise your children, you relive your own childhood, going through (sometimes painfully) the various stages all over again. Then, as a grandparent, you relive your children's lives. The process tends to soften the indignities of aging.

SIX

Macho to Mush

If God had asked Abraham to sacrifice his grandson, he would've said no.

—AUTHOR UNKNOWN

The day after Jordan was born, Aaron and I were in the hospital room when she started her first bout of sustained crying with that piercing, shrill wail that claws at a grandparent's soul. Taylor was still in pain, so Andrew tried soothing the baby, walking her around the room. But that unbearably crushing shriek would not give up. I took Jordan in my arms, certain I could calm her, but alas, she just kept bawling till my skin peeled.

Aaron finally sat down in the rocking chair and said, "Put her on my shoulder." He held her and rocked, and just like that she stopped crying. We joke that there are two benefits to Aaron's having Parkinson's. One is he can eat ice cream or anything he wants all day long and not gain weight; the other is that his soft tremor can put a fussy baby to sleep.

There came a time in 2008 when Aaron, a man of long strides, began walking stiffly and slowly. I noticed his left foot trembling and that his face had become increasingly expressionless. But my mother, Dolly, who also had Parkinson's, was the first to say something. She diagnosed him.

Aaron's doctor put him on dopamine pills, the standard medication for Parkinson's, three or four times a day, and the symptoms subsided, but not entirely. And then he developed a facial tic: his mouth would spasm into uncontrollable contortions. The doctor called it dyskinesia. We would learn that the dopamine pills were causing the dyskinesia, a classic catch-22.

Five months after Jordan was born, Aaron and I were sailing in Nantucket. "Hey, you're not ticcing," I said. "Not at all." It was the first time in over a year.

"I know," he said sheepishly. "I took myself off dopamine."

"What?" As we came about, I shouted into the wind, "You can't do that." If ever he forgot to take those pills, his stiffness and the tremors got worse. "You can't go without dopamine. You need it."

That's when he told me he'd been off the pills for a full week and that his Parkinson's issues had actually lightened so much that he felt symptom-free. And sure enough, he was walking at a normal pace. His scratchy, pinched handwriting was back to its old lovely cursive. Gone was the Parkinsonian mask that froze his smile. He even started driving again. I thought I heard the flap of angels' wings. This was a miracle. It seemed impossible. With Parkinson's, we thought, patients go in only one direction—worse.

We called his doctor, who urged Aaron to stay on dopamine anyway, which he refused to do. He was giddy with renewed vitality.

We had trouble getting a straight explanation for why his symptoms had all but disappeared. One specialist hypothesized he may have had Lyme disease or West Nile virus instead of Parkinson's (not so); another proposed that it was "transient" Parkinson's (whatever that is); yet another said there's such a thing as a disease vacation. My own theory was that becoming a grandfather had healed him.

Being a grandparent can be therapeutic, and I don't say that lightly. I noticed that it had that effect on my *60 Minutes* colleague Bob Simon. The day Bob died in a freak car accident in early 2015 was my worst day in all my years on the show. It was so shocking. You don't expect a guy who spent his life plunging into battlefields from Vietnam to Israel to be felled like that. Other correspondents have died, but they'd been sick (Ed Bradley had leukemia) or they had lived long, full lives (Mike died at ninety-three, Andy at ninety-two). Bob was in the pink of health and at a peak of happiness. He walked out that day to run an errand and never came back.

It hit everyone at *60 Minutes* especially hard. Obviously, it was a loss journalistically, but it hurt more personally. He was a lovable man, full of heart, funny and dashing. It seems that, like me, half the office thought he was their best friend.

And he was full of fun. One day in late 2011, I was distracted by curious sounds coming from his office, adjacent to mine. Was that Bob giggling? I got up and looked in, and there was that grizzled war correspondent down on the floor, rolling around with his four-month-old grandson, Jack.

Up to then Bob had been in a funk for several years, his eyes sad, his walk labored. I knew without being told that he was in the throes of depression, what William Styron called "a storm of murk." I recognized it because Aaron had struggled with depression for years—he called his "the dark pit." Strangely, it was Parkinson's, of all things, that cured Aaron. He had spent years on antidepressants that worked only intermittently. (A new study reports that people with severe depression like Aaron's are at high risk for Parkinson's.) But from the day he went on dopamine, which is a neurotransmitter, he was never depressed again. Catch-23.

Once Jack was born, I noticed that Bob was walking with a new lightness. When we'd pass in the hallway, I'd get a genuine, ready smile. And he had redecorated his office by plastering photos of Jack on every inch of wall space. Some of the pictures were Xeroxes stuck up with Scotch tape. Our boss, Jeff Fager, said it looked like a scene out of *A Beautiful Mind*.

One day I asked Bob if Jack had vanquished his depression. He looked off to think, seeming not to have drawn the connection. "I was still not in good shape when Jack was born."

"Then what?" I pressed. "It went away because of Jack?"

"I guess so. For the first time, Jack brought me joy, which I hadn't experienced in a long time. Now, when I'm with Jack I am happy. Really happy."

I called Dr. David Kahn, a psychiatrist at Columbia University Medical Center in New York, and asked if he'd ever had a case where a grandchild pulled a patient out of the doldrums. He told me about a man in his seventies who, after a long, wildly successful career, suffered a major reversal. He had been a shaker, a one-percenter, a patriarch who supported his family in grand style. But then he lost it all, and became so depressed he was suicidal. Eighty percent of suicides in the United States are by older white men, largely because they're unlikely to seek help.

But this man sought out Dr. Kahn, who concentrated their sessions on finding a reason for him to stay alive. The doctor keyed in on the man's autistic grandson, telling his patient how much the boy needed him. While the grandson was gifted academically, he threw raging tantrums, flapping his hands and banging his head on the wall. Typically socially inept, he had no friends. So at Dr. Kahn's urging, the grandfather started doing things no one else did with the boy, like playing basketball and teaching him how to swim. With the single-minded focus and love of his grandfather, the boy was eventually able to go to a mainstream school and is now at an Ivy League college.

The man never rebuilt his career, but his grandson gave him a powerful motivation to live and restored his capacity to feel joy—and pride. As Dr. Kahn put it, "A suicide was prevented. So yes, grandchildren can be curative in a profound way."

This sent me to Google to see if there'd been any studies. And voilà! An article in the *American Journal of Men's Health* in April 2012 by James Bates and Alan Taylor mentioned research showing that meaningful relationships with grandchildren alleviate depression in men and improve their overall mental health. A study by Sara Moorman presented at the American Sociological

Association's annual meeting in 2013 showed that grandparents who had a close relationship with their older grandchildren complained less of insomnia and lack of energy.

Bob Simon told me that his intense love for his grandson started immediately. "Look, I had Jack—"

"*I* had Jack?" I interrupted.

"That's how I see it, yeah," he said with a smile. "When he wakes up and starts poking at me, it's one of the most exquisite experiences of my life. And every other exquisite experience also has to do with him."

He looked away, then turned back. "There's another dimension too. Which is I guess for anyone over fifty, but particularly people in our game who spend our lives being lied to: being with somebody who is always telling you the truth." Bob paused to chuckle. "There's something so refreshing."

"So very rare," I said, laughing with him.

"Jack has become the most important thing in my life." He sighed. "I had no idea. I had no idea what it would be."

"It's all a huge surprise, this grandchild business, right?"

"That's almost an understatement. It's a turning point. It's a pivotal event. And there aren't many of those."

There are grandpas whose faces lighten at the mere mention of their grandchild. On September 8, 2014, George W. Bush and Bill Clinton were interviewed together at a Presidential Leadership Scholars program. Clinton was about to become a grandfather and Bush was asked to give him some advice: "Be prepared to fall completely in love again. You're not going to believe it."

Bush looked at Clinton and laughed. "You're just not going to believe the joy, and the fun. And oh yeah, get ready to be like the lowest person in the pecking order in your family!"

John McCain, former Republican nominee for president and longtime senator, was close to sappy when I asked him about being a grandfather.

"I have four," he said with a grin, softening.

I've written about the grandmother gaze. Well, grandpas have one too. Just talking about their grandchildren, their jaws unclench, shoulders relax. Get their minds on those kids and even Super Hawk (McCain's nickname in the Senate) turns into a lambkin.

"You know, my POW buddies are dying," he said. "You hear that clock ticking and you find yourself appreciating flowers." He cast me a can-you-believe-it? smile. "I never used to stop to look at flowers or sunrises or birds."

I was taken by his vigor. I saw no sign that his age, seventy-eight, was slowing him down physically or mentally. But he was telling me he was, shall we say, ripening, and being a grandfather was a contributing factor.

"You get more sensitive when you're a grandfather. And you think more about your legacy. You realize your heritage rests with those babies."

Linda Fried, dean of the Mailman School of Public Health at Columbia, told me, "For a lot of men, being a grandparent is the most important thing that ever happened to them. The moment that child is born, what I have seen repeatedly, it's like a gene gets flicked on. They suddenly get this surge of love they never had, altruistic love they never experienced before. I can't explain it: it's just love. Seems to bring out this great need to secure their own legacy in these children."

There are, of course, grandfathers who don't give a hoot. Some simply can't abide the noise—"the wild Indians"—and the diapers. They have no patience with little babies. But in my admittedly unscholarly survey, I found mostly enthusiasm. Aaron, for instance, would get an oohey-gooey look when he held Jordan. He was so blown over when she was born that he said it was like his dad used to say in Spur: "I feel like throwin' my hat over the windmill!"

I asked Aaron and the other grandfathers I interviewed if they had felt a full-body electric surge when they first held the baby, and not one said yes, whereas all but a few of the women knew just what I was talking about.

"When Jordan was born," Aaron said, "my emotions were all tied up with my daughter having a child. I think I loved the baby so much because I love Taylor so much."

My old friend and colleague Eric Engberg told me his reaction was tinged with worry. He and I covered the White House together for CBS during the Reagan administration. "The thing you'll hear from fathers, I suspect," said Eric, "is the same feeling I had, which is not so much, 'Gee, I'm a grandfather now,' as 'I hope this son of mine doesn't screw this up.'" He said he'd seen his son through the first twenty-five years of his life. "I've paid his parking tickets and I've been to the teachers' conferences where they were asking, 'Why doesn't this kid study hard?' You've bailed this kid outta trouble and you know he's not perfect. You just pray he gets this—being a dad—right."

Several of the grandfathers I spoke to were taken by surprise, like the chairman of the Joint Chiefs. Martin Dempsey may have been militaristic by background and bearing, but he told me that when his first grandchild was born, "It just brought me to my knees, you know, with emotion."

I caught up with Dempsey at a national security conference in Aspen, Colorado, and asked if he could articulate why he was so moved. I thought he'd give me a good answer since he has a master's degree in Irish poetry.

"There's that sense of immortality and mortality all at the same time. Immortality in that your offspring will persist into the future, and mortality when you remind yourself, 'Oh my God, I'm a grandfather!' You know, there's no such thing as a young grandfather." He was fifty-five when the first of his eight grandkids was born.

As with grandmothers, how a paw paw responds to becoming a grandfather seems to depend on how old he is when the grandchild is born. Say Grandpa's in his forties. While he could be more hands-on, more active with his grandchild, he's still busy building his career and doesn't have much time. And he very likely cringes at the idea of being "that old" so soon.

Unlike women, men don't typically long to be a grandparent, so with them there's often the "What? I'm a grandfather? Where'd that come from?" factor. Men today can and do get face-lifts, Botox shots, lip plumpings with Restylane filler, liposuction, hair transplants, facials and eyebrow waxes; they hire personal trainers and nutritionists and get shots of human growth hormone. Vanity, thy name is man. *Anything* to stay fit—and look young.

And then one day the phone call comes: "Dad, guess what? I'm pregnant." Holy crap. Me? A Barcalounging, hairy-eared codger, me? This cannot be.

Men in their sixties and seventies have thought they'd be forever young. To them, the specter of grampa-ness means the death of vitality, snap and sex. There is no glimmer that having a grandchild is a new beginning.

One day Tom Brokaw and I were in a delicatessen on Madison Avenue, reminiscing. We've known each other since 1968, when we both covered Bobby Kennedy's campaign for president, Tom as an NBC correspondent, I as an NBC researcher.

"So did you go through the 'How can I be a grandfather? This is crazy?' thing?" I ask.

"Well, yeah. It passed through my mind, though I didn't resist." He gave me a crooked smile, and I thought, Still so handsome. He was fifty-seven when his first grandchild—a girl—was born. "Meredith"—Tom's wife—"immediately said, 'She can call me Nan.' And I said, 'So I get to be "Grandpa"? I don't think so.'" He looked at me slyly. "They all call me Tom."

He made sure I realized that he's not technically a boomer, since, like me, he was born just before the start of the population bulge. He's in the pre-boomer grandfather fraternity along with rockers like Paul Simon, Keith Richards and Mick Jagger, who's a grandfather *and* a great-grandfather. Famous boomer grandfathers include Tom Hanks, Jim Carrey, Donny Osmond, Steven Tyler and now of course Bill Clinton.

Unlike so many successful men who retire, Tom, now in his midseventies, has managed his post-top-of-the-mountain life with grace, turning himself from a network anchorman into an accomplished bestselling author and elder statesman. And he let his hair turn white.

"So, Tom," I asked when our breakfast arrived, "what about this I'm-too-young-to-be-a-granddaddy?" He told me two stories:

The first was about a guy he knew who wanted his grandson to call him Ben. So, it was Grandparents' Day at preschool and Ben walks in. Little Neddy looks up and says, "Ben, what are you doing here?" And Ben says, "It's Grandparents' Day. I'm your grandfather." And little Neddy says, "You are?"

The other story was about Tom's pal Robert Redford. They were in Sundance, coming out of Redford's restaurant. "The people, if they know that he's around, kind of gather outside to take a look," said Tom. "So Bob comes out, and he's full Bob, you know. He's got the suede shirt, the cowboy boots and the whole thing."

The gawkers were trying not to be obvious about it, but their necks were craning. Redford strutted down the street in full sex symbol swagger, and as Tom tells it, "About ten feet behind him are these two darling redheaded munchkins running up shouting, 'Grandpa Bob, Grandpa Bob.'" Tom laughed and laughed. "Bob looks at me, and he looks at them, and he says loud enough for everybody to hear, 'Not in public, kids. Not in public.'"

If you don't become a grandparent till you're older, like Aaron and me, in our sixties, all that "When did *this* happen?" business goes away. You never say, "Oh, I'm too young." What you do say is:

"When the hell is this ever going to happen? And will I be healthy, vigorous and fun enough?"

Another colleague at *60 Minutes*, Morley Safer, was seventy when his first grandchild was born. "I looked at this little scrunched-up thing and surprised myself with how emotional I felt. I welled up," he told me.

But there's a dark side to being as old as he was. "There's the regret of not getting married earlier and having your own kids earlier," he said. "You won't be around to see them succeed and see them do the right thing, be people with good character." He made me sad.

But at least Morley has grandchildren. If you get to seventy and none of your kids have kids, you may get desperate and start offering incentives (bribes), like paying for fertility treatments. I've heard of parents paying up to $30,000 for their daughters to freeze their eggs, so that if all else fails they can go in for in vitro fertilization and become a single parent.

Aaron and I sometimes ask each other, "What is a grandfather supposed to be, besides a wizard?" Dr. James Bates, an expert in family studies at Ohio State, is one of the few who has researched the subject. He says that grandfathers can be important in giving grandchildren a sense of identity and confidence. "A grandfather should tell the kids stories about himself as a boy, how he grew up—in a way that allows him to talk about perseverance and sacrifice. He should describe the family's roots and traditions. Kids need to know what it's like to be part of a family and have a connection to the past."

Grampa should joke around. He should be a mentor, passing on practical skills like how to throw a basketball or shoot a gun. Though he's likely to confront something of a role reversal. It used to be gramps taught kids skills; nowadays it's the kids who teach gramps how to take a picture on an iPhone!

Grampa is often a sounding board and a confidant who comforts during difficult times. Kids often find Grampa is less judgmental, so they feel freer to confide in him and ask personal questions about sensitive issues. He's that person to go to when times at home get tough. There's something about older men: they can be more lenient and tolerant and calming. The main thing, though, for a granddad is simply "being there."

Relationships with grandfathers usually grow stronger as children age. Kids tend to prefer Gramma at first, but then things even out. In polls, teenage boys name their grandfathers as the family member they "get on best with." In some cases, as the grandchildren get older, they withdraw from their grandmothers. I know several who talk about a veil of sadness that descends when their teenage grandchildren begin expressing their independence. "They don't call as much. They have their own friends, their own lives." Some grannies and pops go to great lengths to plan summer vacations grandchildren cannot resist. I met a CEO who has ten grandchildren. As each one turns sixteen, she takes them on a trip of their choosing. She's gone from the outback in Australia to a fashion show in Paris, neither one on her bucket list. It reminds me of something Tom Brokaw said: "For parents, bribery is a white-collar crime; for grandparents, it's a business plan!"

Now, this is purely anecdotal (again, from my own survey), but it seems older grandsons like to move in with Pops. Take my old boss Bill Small, the CBS Washington bureau chief who hired me. He's had two of his grandsons as roommates. First Jesse, now thirty and a vice president at Goldman Sachs. "He's Felix Unger," Bill deadpanned. After his wife, Gish, died, Jesse moved in—just for a few weeks to keep Grandpa company—then stayed for four years. When he moved to his own apartment half a block away, his younger brother Elias moved in. "He's at NYU," Bill gloated, "and a really good cook." Their mother, Bill's daughter Tami, told me: "It's not unusual for me to go to the apartment and find them both in my dad's bed rooting for the Yankees and snacking on a bowl of something that's not on my dad's cardio diet."

When I watched Andrew toss Jordan around, flipping her upside down in the air, I thought: That's exactly the way Aaron used to play with Taylor. Turns out boisterous scuffle-play is programmed into dads and granddads: they are precoded to swing babies in the air. According to Louann Brizendine, the roughhousing "makes kids more curious, improves their ability to learn, and gives them self-confidence." After Brizendine wrote *The Female Brain,* she wrote *The Male Brain,* in which she says the free-wheeling toss-and-tickle play, the wrestling and pillow fighting, teach kids how to settle down when they get overexcited. Unlike the more naturally protective Mom, Dad allows the child to explore and take risks. And when men engage in the rough-and-tumble, the close physical contact releases oxytocin (yes, in dads too) and other hormones inducing feelings of pleasure, bonding the relationship. It slays me every time I am reminded that we are all just bags of chemicals.

Taylor has spun Jordan around like an airplane; I have too. When moms and grannies do horseplay, the child will learn the same things. But dads and granddads do it more often, and for longer stretches.

Little girls tend to tire of the rowdiness and will divert Gramps by making him role-play. One grandmother friend told me, "It's like a lightning bolt hit my husband. Oh, listen, when I saw him on the floor playin' Barbies with our granddaughter, I thought I'd faint." Same for me when I saw Aaron folded up on one of Jordan's kiddie chairs sipping her invisible tea and chewing on her "This is so good!" imaginary chocolate cake.

Dads are more creative and goofier than moms. Brizendine says that when dads sing "Itsy Bitsy Spider," they're more likely to improvise new verses; they're definitely more stimulating. And they're more likely to engage in teasing, which improves their kids' ability to guess what's on another person's mind and to recognize mental tricks and deceits. A father or grandfather's unpredictability helps children to be brave in different situations or when meeting new people. It's said that girls who were the most popular in school enjoyed playing with their fathers or grandfathers.

And grandfathers love fooling around with their grandkids. Take Franklin Roosevelt with "his iridescent personality," as Winston Churchill described him. "Meeting Franklin Roosevelt," Churchill once said, "was like opening your first bottle of champagne; knowing him was like drinking it." While Eleanor left much of the mothering and grandmothering to her mother-in-law, Franklin adored playing with his thirteen grandchildren. He had slides, swings and sandboxes built for them on the South Lawn of the White House.

FDR would begin his presidential workday not in the Oval Office, but upstairs in the living quarters, with his close aides arrayed around his bed, while he finished with his breakfast tray. His grandson Curtis said it was "more like a *levée* of Louis XIV than a twentieth-century staff briefing."

Curtis, called Buzzie, and his sister moved into the White House in 1933 with their mother, Anna, when she got divorced. The two little ones would burst into FDR's bedroom in the morning and disrupt the agenda with loud squeals "greeted with equal noise by [their] grandfather," Curtis says. He and his sister would hop up onto the double bed, one on either side of the president of the United States. All work would stop so "Papa" could lavish them with the kind of affection Eleanor was so woefully incapable of. He would read the funnies out loud, like a comedian, and leave everyone in stitches.

"My grandfather seemed to savor the few minutes of silliness with my sister and me as much as we did . . . The fact that the occasional morning visitors—like Dean Acheson, then assistant secretary of the treasury, who had to set the price of gold every day with the president's approval—were not equally amused by such playful goings-on didn't trouble FDR."

Other men of that era were caught in the downdraft of the Depression, which tended to snuff out their energy and playfulness.

It made them remote and inaccessible. Aaron told me, "My grandfather was distant. I can't remember that we had any relationship. But he whittled little animals for me, and he gave me his fiddle."

I knew only my paternal grandfather, Harry Stahl, whom everyone called Boss. He was anything but aloof and unapproachable. I remember how soft his eyes would get when he looked at me, his first grandchild. He would kiss me and toss me around, pretending he was going to drop me. I loved him and knew he loved me. The same with my grandmother Esther, though she was sickly and died when I was fairly young. My mother said she never recovered from the death of her youngest child, my uncle Jake, in the war.

Harry and Esther grew up together in Poland, where he was a lumberjack in Wlodawa (pronounced Vla-dava) and helped in his mother's small grocery store. When he was a boy, the family had enough money to buy just one violin, which was given to the oldest son, Nathan, along with music lessons. The rest of the kids, eight in all, carved their own instruments and became a forest orchestra, Nathan teaching the others how to play.

Harry and Esther came to Boston via Liverpool in 1913 to join Nathan, the first to make the pilgrimage. Everyone in the Stahl family except their father followed, one or two at a time, most of them settling near Harry on the North Shore of Massachusetts. When Grampa got here, the folks at immigration read his name, Heinach, and told him he was Harry. When his younger brother Hershel came years later after World War I, he too was given the name Harry. So Grampa was Big Harry, and his baby brother was Little Harry.

My grandfather started his own business making dyes for

leather: first just black and oxblood, later red, white and blue. The company, called Stahl Finish, survived the Depression and then thrived once World War II started. The military bought millions of shoes, boots and jackets, all made of leather.

Neither Big Harry nor any of his brothers or sisters ever wanted to go back to Poland, even as tourists. But I did. So in late September 2012, I flew to Warsaw with my cousins, who adored Grampa as much as I did. We wanted to see where he grew up.

There were six of us: Aaron and me, and cousins Patty Stahl, a psychologist in Dallas, and her husband, Chet Morrison; and Jim Stahl, a playwright and magazine publisher in Rhode Island, and his wife, Maryann.

We checked into the Vanilla Hotel in Lublin, home to forty thousand Jews at the beginning of World War II. Today, we were told, there are none. We walked around the old Jewish quarter, newly renovated for tourists, passing a school where seven-year-olds were up on an outdoor stage, singing and performing for Grandparents' Day.

We strolled past lovely two-story buildings in Mediterranean pastels, with ornate gables like the canal houses in Amsterdam. Some of the façades were covered with giant photographs, blow-ups from a stash hidden away in 1939 and found only recently. They were portraits by a professional photographer of local middle-class Jews, posing in pearls and finery. They all looked so happy and secure; they had no idea what was about to happen to them.

When the Nazis came, they smashed everything and sent all the Jews either to Sobibor to be gassed, or to a nearby work camp, Majdanek. Slav, our guide, blamed the Germans. Grampa had always blamed the Poles.

On the second day of our visit Slav drove us to the countryside to find Wlodawa. On the way Aaron read a "Welcome to Kaplonospy" sign and said, "We're in Colonoscopy!" "Been there," said Jim, making us howl with laughter. Jim is like a handsome Oxford don: tweedy, soft-spoken and droll. Patty has a mop of unruly blond curls and a merry sense of humor. I can't think of better company.

I was not expecting to see much in Wlodawa. We'd been told that the Germans destroyed everything Jewish. Every building, every record, every scrap of paper. They even tore up the gravestones and used them to pave the roads.

Unlike Warsaw with its tall, modern buildings and trendy European shops, Wlodawa was frozen, intact from the early 1900s. When we got to the center of town we found a local guide, Chris, who took us to the synagogue. There it was, still standing from back then. Chris told us the Nazis decided not to tear it down, so they could use it to store military matériel. It was an enormous white churchlike structure with two large buildings from the same period on either side: one, Chris said, was the old yeshiva.

"Grampa was here," said Patty with tears in her eyes. I followed her into the chapel to try to commune with Harry's ghost. It was a big, empty space with an ornate ark at one end but no pews. Of course. No congregants.

We never dreamed we would actually stand in the place where Grampa was Bar Mitzvahed, and, we assumed, married. But Chris said they would have been married outside, since women weren't allowed in the chapel. "They were here. I'm sure of it," said Patty again. I felt it too.

In the foyer, Aaron found a rack of black-and-white photos of

Wlodawa at the turn of the twentieth century. We were transfixed, imagining Grampa walking along the streets, into the market.

We had one address: that of Grampa's uncle Velvel, who had lived on Mill Street. (When he came to the United States, he became Bill Stile.) We couldn't believe our eyes: one of the photos was of Milgas (or Mill) Street. The guide told us it was still there, just a short walk from the synagogue. It was lined with small one-story bungalows, exactly the ones in the old photo. They all looked pretty much the same, so we picked one and declared, "It's Uncle Velvel's!"

Sobibor was next door, a walk—a march—away. The Nazis turned it into a crematorium. While Grampa's family had left decades before the war, our grandmother's hadn't, so when the war ended, Harry hired someone to search for her relatives. Only two nephews had survived, and that was because they had been freedom fighters who lived in the forest, much like the men in *Inglourious Basterds*.

We walked to the Bug River, which we guessed was the route of escape from Wlodawa to the Baltic Sea, and then west to Liverpool. This was what we had come for: to breathe the same air our grandparents had, walk their streets, imbibe our past. "I can't believe we found it," I said, my voice shaking. Even in the shadow of the Holocaust, we were happy.

In my research on grandfathers, I learned about the changing definition of the ideal husband. Men who were born early in the twentieth century grew up during the First World War and fought in the Second. They had a special status, looked up to as heroes. Being a man meant being the breadwinner; for the most part they left child-rearing to the little woman.

My dad and Aaron's dad, both of that generation, were marshmallows when it came to their grandchildren. One of my favorite pictures is of my father whirling little Taylor up in the air, the seventy-year-old and the seven-month-old laughing together without inhibition. Taylor remembers Lulu, as she called him, teaching her (his first grandchild) to swim and maneuver a boat around Marblehead Harbor. Taylor was the only grandchild of Aaron's father, Clyde. Clyde was what we used to call strapping: six foot five (taller than Aaron), with hands the size of bear paws. And there he was with Tay on his lap, both of them buried under a pile of her stuffed animals. He taught her how to drive a golf cart, when she was seven.

The sons of that World War II generation, basically the boomers, grew up under very different circumstances. Their war was Vietnam—hardly seen as heroic—and their big domestic battles were over the women's rights movement and affirmative action, both of which propelled women into the workplace. By necessity, husbands became more attentive dads. They didn't vacuum or shop for groceries, but they played with their kids and took them to Little League. Some, like Aaron, became coaches.

In 1992 Aaron wrote an article about this for *M* magazine called "Fathering the Nest: The New American Manhood." To be a successful dad, he wrote, "American fathers are going to have to learn to talk about emotions, become nurturers as well as providers."

And men did change, along with society. As Aaron wrote, hos-

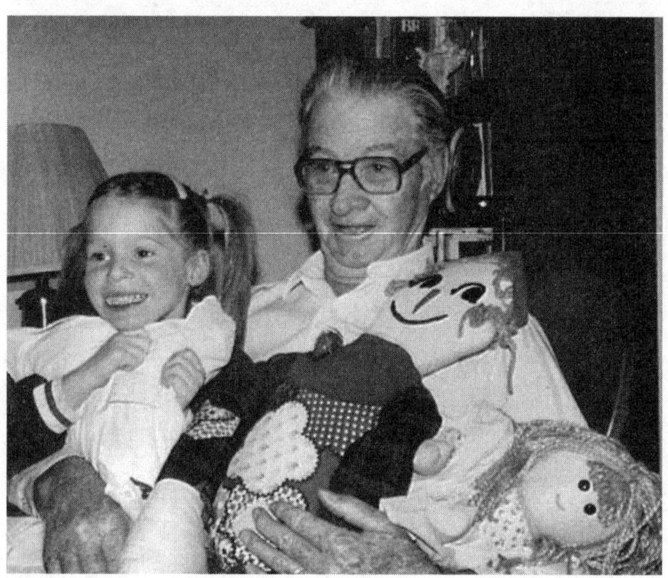

TOP *My father, Louis, playing with Taylor, 1978.*
BOTTOM *Taylor and my father-in-law, Clyde, 1981.*

pitals began offering new fathers counseling to help with their postpartum depression; baby-changing tables popped up in the men's rooms at train stations and airports. Television began to reflect the change with shows about devoted dads like *The Cosby Show*. And Madison Avenue created ads with men as homebodies: a Dawn commercial featured a dad washing dishes with his preschooler.

Those fathers who had their kids in the late 1970s and '80s are today's grandfathers. The walls of their living rooms are covered with pictures of grandkids asleep in Pop's arms or on his lap being read to.

The grandpa mellowing has been facilitated by something called "andropause," the male equivalent of menopause. In their prime, men are men because of three hormones, says Louann Brizendine. Testosterone builds all that is "male," including the compulsion to outrank other males; vasopressin, the so-called gallantry chemical, makes men protectors of turf, mates and children, and is also responsible for male bonding; and MSH (known as the de-feminizer) strips away all that is female.

Men generally go through andropause between the ages of fifty and sixty-five. During this stage those male-hormone levels decline, estrogen increases, and so does our old friend oxytocin, known in men as the "Down, boy" hormone. This is "the closest that men will ever come to being like women," says Brizendine, "since oxytocin makes them more open to affection and sentiment, and declining testosterone makes them less aggressive." It's why, she says, the love circuits in the granddaddy brain can be "hijacked by the adorable little Tommy, even more than they had

Aaron and Jordan at the beach in Nantucket, 2013.

been when [his son] was born. . . . He was amused by everything his grandson did and said," and he has more patience than he had with his own kids.

If it's all about chemistry, then how come grampas of old weren't nurturing? Because andropause was rare until fairly recently. Men didn't live long enough. Even in the early twentieth century, the average age of death for men in the United States was forty-five. It's a fairly new phenomenon that men live decades after those masculine hormones start to recede.

This made me curious: do men undergo their own progression of biochemical fluctuations and rewirings when they become fathers? In her book, Brizendine says yes, that a man's brain changes with his wife's pregnancy. For instance, close to two-thirds of expectant fathers exhibit symptoms of pregnancy, like weight gain and morning sickness. After the birth, their testosterone can sink by a third, reducing their sex drive. At the same time, the new dad's estrogen levels increase, and perhaps most astonishing, they have a rise in prolactin, the lactation hormone. Sometimes, in doing research you learn things you didn't really want to know.

The median age for new grandfathers in the United States is fifty-four (for grandmothers, fifty), though the number is rising, since many in our generation waited to have our kids, and they're waiting to have theirs. In Third World countries you see grandpas as young as twenty-eight, and even in this country there are pockets where they're thirty-five. Grandfathers that young tend to be poor, struggling with a job (if they have one) and possibly still raising their own kids. The image of a grandfather leisurely playing with grandkids is a privileged one. As with much in our society today, grandparenthood has become polarized by class.

This is something Dick Beattie brought up. I first met Dick, who looks strikingly like the actor Ed Harris, when he was general counsel at what was then called the Department of Health, Education and Welfare (HEW) in the Carter administration. Today, as a lawyer in New York, he admonished me not to look at men in Manhattan (like him) as anything close to the norm. "There's been so much wealth made here in the last thirty years, it's distorting," he said. "This city's such a narrow sliver when you look at the country as a whole." His point is obviously well taken. But we agreed that whatever one's financial circumstances, being a "good grandparent" depends more on one's physical and mental health and emotional commitment than on one's bank account.

The reason I wanted to talk to Dick was that I had heard he walked his granddaughters to school every day. A high-powered mergers and acquisitions attorney, he's the head of Simpson Thacher, yet there he was boarding a bus every morning with two little girls and holding their hands as they crossed the streets on their way to nursery school, then kindergarten. "Did that every day," he said. "You tell me a better way to start the day than being with your grandchildren."

I hadn't seen or talked to Eric Engberg in years. When he sent me a clipping about a book he thought I should read, I called to thank him. Hearing his rich, deep voice—he sounds like a radio announcer, even off the air—brought back a memory: he had taken early retirement from CBS and moved to Bradenton, Florida, so he and his wife, Judy, could live near their grandchildren. He wanted to be in their lives.

"Well, we moved for the kids—and our boat," he said with a chuckle. "We live near the water down here. But we're not unusual. We have lots of friends who, when the husbands retired, came down here to be near their grandkids."

That's something of a trend these days, older couples pulling up roots—selling their houses, packing up years of accumulated junk (or selling it or burning it) and moving across the country so they can watch their grandbabies grow up.

I asked Eric if he would gather a group of those friends together for a chat. One Saturday in March 2012, I flew into Tampa and drove an hour or so to Bradenton, a town of clean streets, middle-class houses and an armada of boats.

I met with Eric, Judy, and six of their friends over lunch (people talk about doing "legwork" when they research a project; I did "gullet work") in a small conference room at the local Hampton Inn.

"I'm Dick Palmeroy," one of the men began, "retired from an air-conditioning company. Was in sales for thirty-eight years. And this is my wife, Patsy." Good-looking. That's the first thing I thought about him, and her.

"Do you like being retired?" I asked Dick.

"Love it. I play golf with my buddies two, three times a week." And he looked it. Trim and tan, with barely any streaks of gray in his thick head of hair. "We have Kayden—that's our grandson—one day a week. He's almost three. We have him on Tuesday. Our day is Tuesday," he chortled. They had moved there from

Mississippi to live twenty minutes away from Kayden and his baby sister.

Like me, Patsy said she had waited and waited to have a grandchild, and not that patiently. "I told our two sons, 'You better hurry up and have the grandchildren before you're changin' their diapers and mine too!'" The whole table broke into appreciative laughter. "It's difficult to be a grandmother today," she went on. "There's a hole in my tongue from biting it so often." That produced a round of "know what ya mean" head nods.

Patsy's a cross between a philosopher and a stand-up comic. She told the group, with a straight face, "God created Eve because Adam was drivin' him crazy asking him so many questions. 'What do I do with this, God?' 'Where did I leave that, God?'"

Patsy had been a school administrator for years. She too glowed with hardiness, even with her puff of white Barbara Bush hair. In her case she looked younger than her husband, with her fashionable hoop earrings and perfectly drawn eyeliner.

"Dick wasn't there that much when we raised our two boys. Now, though, we have Kayden, and he can see him every day. But Dick's not used to things like the terrible twos. It's hard for these men to deal with tantrums, unlike Grandma. We know that it's okay." I guess she was referring to the feeling "I just want to smack the little bugger."

"They've got so much stuff," said Eric Engberg. "They used to come to visit with their Xboxes and their ray guns and they don't wanna play with you at all. They wanna sit down with their stuff—when they're old enough to use an Xbox, which I guess is probably five, right?" I didn't interrupt to point out that most of that "stuff" was bought by us, the grandparents.

Eric looked pretty much the same as he had in his White House years, except for a little extra poundage around the middle and a few wisps of white hair fringing his sideburns.

"Our oldest son, who married his college sweetheart, had two little ones in a row," he said. "When the youngest was a year old, and his brother three, somethin' like that, I retired and came here. Judy and I really looked forward to a storybook lifestyle of seeing our grandchildren a lot and using our boat a lot. And that was the case for the first four or five years. We babysat for them quite a bit."

Judy looked down. "We'd be with them on the holidays," Eric went on. "I used to play with the little girl; write her a special note on Christmas Eve from Santa Claus. Once I purposely put in a misspelling and she noticed. She said, 'What happened here, Grandpa?' And I said, 'I think one of those reindeer took over the note writing. And you know the reindeer are stupid. They're not like Santa.' And she said, which I'll never forget, 'He was doing his best.' That's the kinda stuff that melts your heart and you remember forever."

We were eating salads and chicken on rice. A pitcher of iced tea was on the table. Eric began talking about how much he loves his grandchildren and how terrifying it is when they get sick. "We had a kid once, I don't remember which one, who was running a tremendous fever—a hundred and six degrees—and they couldn't get it down. I said to Judy, 'Man, you don't know the meaning of the words "I'm scared" until you have a child.' Right? And then you have a grandchild who gets some kind of illness or has some other problem, and you go through the exact same set of fear patterns. It's like somebody dumped the responsibilities of parenthood on you all over again twenty-five years later—but you don't have any control. Although, I don't know, that never seemed to bother me that much." He was smiling. "The fact that, you know, I wasn't in charge."

The lunch was a jolly afternoon of storytelling until Eric veered off course. He had more to tell us about his move to Florida. "Our dream in Bradenton ended because my son lost his job." You could feel the mood shift. Everyone stopped eating. "He was a civil engineer, involved in building highways, and that was one of the first things to die when the recession hit."

"Yeah," I said, "Florida was hit hard."

"It sure was," Eric said. "He was unemployed for at least a year and a half. Depression and fear and anxiety caused him to start drinking. And his wife couldn't stand that, so eventually, she decided to divorce him."

I had not expected this at all. And from the expressions around the table, this was news to his other friends as well.

"That happened about four years ago." He looked over at Judy. "As a result, we barely ever see the grandchildren anymore. And it's not that she—our daughter-in-law—is trying to keep us from the kids. It's that she's gotta work to support herself and her children. So she moved to Tampa."

Judy hadn't said a word. It occurred to me that she had already done her crying years back and was now resigned to the situation, much like a widow.

"But if you *wanted* to see them?" I asked her.

"The kids are now teenagers," said Judy. "They're fifteen and thirteen. So they're very busy with their own . . ." She trailed off.

When I had arranged the lunch, I was expecting to only hear about the joys of proximity, the recuperative happiness of seeing grandchildren every day. Now I was reminded that not seeing them can puncture your heart.

"Hey," said Eric, trying to lighten things up, "we still have our boat."

Eric has plenty of company in the "grandchildren pilgrimage didn't work out the way we planned" department. I know of cases where after the grandparents have moved across the country, their kids have had to relocate for their job. One of the women at the Bradenton lunch confided that her daughter had stopped talking to her and no longer allowed her to see her granddaughter. So it's not just daughters-in-law who do the cutting off. I'm told when it's your own child slamming the door, it's even more excruciating.

But most of the grandparent stories I have come across are about soul enrichment and hot-diggity loving. One couple of codgers had been living together for years. They saw no reason to get married and merge their Social Security checks. But then he became a grandfather, and they raced off to Vegas to elope and make it legitimate. "Living in sin" was no longer fitting.

The most unusual story I've heard is that of my new friend B. Siperstein. When B.'s first two grandchildren were born, he was Barry, their grandpa, known as Pop Pop. Now B.'s their grandma. She's Babs. Babs is a transgender grandparent. (I'm told saying "tranny granny" would not be appreciated.)

"What do they call you now?" I asked.

"Still Pop Pop."

We were having lunch (of course) at Gabriel's on West Sixtieth Street, near my office. Babs was conservatively dressed in a plain blouse and cardigan over black pants. She's attractive—very attractive—in a grandmotherly kind of way, wearing a wig, pale lipstick and simple hoop earrings. She displayed not a hint of masculinity, even in her hands.

When Babs was Barry, he ran a family paint business, had a mustache, loved sports and raised three children with his wife, Carol. He was in his early fifties when he broached the subject of his gender identity with Carol. Babs's daughter Jana told me that her mom was cooking Sunday pancakes and sausages when her dad first brought the subject up. "Mom dropped the skillet on the floor."

But Carol accepted his decision to change, and more. She helped him through the process, including painful electrolysis and Adam's apple shaving. She taught him how to dress and walk. They decided to stay together, married, as two women. It was their own *Modern Family*.

Babs told me there was no family trauma to her conversion, "because I had a very long transition."

But when I checked that out with her daughter, she said, "Maybe compared to other families. I've heard serious horror stories." It was easy for her, she said, "but my older brothers had problems. I think it's harder for men to accept this." She told me there were zero issues for Babs's grandchildren. "Yeah, she's still Pop Pop, but they're wonderful with her."

"What do you call Babs?" I asked.

"Dad. She's my father and that'll never change."

Sadly, Carol died a few years ago. "That's when I became both a grandfather and a grandmother," said Babs.

Her two older grandchildren, now fifteen and thirteen, live in Florida, while she lives in New Jersey. "For years my son was concerned every time I'd go down there. He was afraid I'd do the big splash." So she would dress in understated, unisex outfits. But by now everyone's accepted the change.

"Did you have the operation?" I asked.

"Yes, I'm fully trans," said Babs. "But I still have to take hormones."

Babs is now a political activist, the first transgender member of the Democratic National Committee. She still runs the family paint business, along with her daughter Jana, who's expecting a baby. Babs is planning the shower with the mother-in-law-to-be. "This'll be something new. I've never even been to a baby shower.

"I'm essentially the same person," she tells me, "still attracted to women, though I have a different point of view since I've been on both sides." That, she says, makes her a better grandparent since she understands both boys and girls, can see their issues from both perspectives.

Over dessert and coffee, she joked, "I describe myself as someone who's been scarred by many years of testosterone!" Babs has a lovely smile. I had a great time with her. We were two gabbing grandmothers, swapping stories.

And then there are the classic cases of second chances, of grandfathers who were busy when their own children were growing up and want a new turn at the plate.

When I interviewed Tom Brokaw he told me, "We got married when Meredith was twenty-one and I was twenty-two. And we had three kids—bang, bang, bang—before we were thirty."

"So I guess you feel having grandchildren gives you a chance to be more involved," I said.

"Yeah, it does," he said. "With my children, I was too busy chasing my career and traveling to have a lot of time to spend with them. But now I can make up for that with my grandchildren."

Tom has five grandchildren. Two of the girls live around the corner from him in New York City—"We have Thursdays with them." He has two other granddaughters in San Francisco and one grandson, an infant, in LA. When he's not writing books or making documentaries for NBC, he's on a loop of grandchildren outings, from New York to California to Montana.

Munching on an English muffin, Tom told me he's completely engrossed in the kids, totally different from his own grandfather. "For one thing, I can talk to all four of our granddaughters about common interests. Our tastes are the same, even our wardrobes. Grandparents wear the same running shoes. And we like the same music. There's this convergence of interest and taste."

His newest baby, Archer Thomas Merritt Brokaw, was just over a year old. Tom's youngest daughter, Sarah, was forty-two and unmarried when one day she announced to her parents: "I'm going to have a baby. I've picked out the sperm donor." *Modern Family,* Brokaw-style. Sarah told Tom and Meredith that the donor was a Chinese-American friend. "He's athletic, an architect, and gay. And oh, smart and a great guy." That was that.

"So she has the baby, a year and two months ago," Tom says, his grandpa eyes beaming. "The kid is unbelievable."

Tom and Meredith moved out to Los Angeles before Archer was born to help Sarah set up: buy the crib, changing table, receiving blankets and diapers. And to be there for the birth. "I got weepy," said Tom, "and I thought, What a life we've had, you know. But it doesn't get any better than this."

Sarah was alone, no partner, no second pair of hands. So they stayed on. "Yeah, Meredith and I took a place near them for two months and it worked out perfectly. We lived a bike ride away." They were the ones who stood in so Sarah could sleep. For Tom, it was total-immersion grandfathering.

"All the other stuff that goes on in our lives," he said, "but this is what really moves you." He reached into his pocket, pulled out his iPhone and showed me picture after picture of Archer.

It all gets back to the idea of us grandparents being there to help our overwhelmed kids with child care. Here's something I found out about older grandfathers: if they're retired, they're not only available, they're eager to babysit. Often their wives are younger and haven't retired yet. The men who haven't figured out what to do with themselves are becoming—well, let's call them RGNs, Retired Grandfather Nannies.

I heard about this at my lunch with economist Betsey Stevenson of the president's Council of Economic Advisers. "I rely on my father more than my mother to help us," she told me. "My mom's still working and my dad isn't. And my dad is patient with young children in a way Mom isn't."

When Betsey was growing up, her parents had traditional gender roles. "My mom changed the diapers and took care of the babies and my dad went to work. He stayed in the waiting room during the delivery." But everything changed when he retired. He plunged into his second chance. "He's the one who went with me to have my ultrasounds. He was really excited. He'd never seen an ultrasound before."

When I met with her, Betsey had only recently moved to Washington. Her daughter, Mathilda, was four. "It was my dad who came down from Boston and stayed with us for three weeks to help Mathilda with the transition, which included a new school."

Betsey went on: "For a lot of grandfathers this is their first time to play an active role as a caregiver. We should make as much space for them to do that as possible. Men particularly struggle when they retire. They scramble to figure out their place in society. Being an active grandparent, a caregiving grandparent, is a real role. It can make a lot of grandfathers feel fulfilled."

I don't often read the sports section of the paper, but I do love to watch football on Sundays. I'm a fan of the New York Giants, but when the camera sits on Tom Coughlin, the longtime coach, I turn to Aaron and say: "What a sourpuss. He's either scowling or throwing a two-year-old's hissy fit. What's with the uncontrollable rage in that guy?" As Billy Witz wrote in the *New York Times*, he's "a ranter, arm waver . . . his face perpetually red from exhortation, irritation and unyielding determination."

But Witz reported that in his tenth season as coach, Coughlin had become more subdued, "more likely to commend than condemn." Witz wondered if he had toned it down because he won a second Super Bowl championship in 2012.

Coughlin's wife, Judy, said that wasn't it. "Grandkids have softened him. He wasn't around for our kids a lot of the time, and when he was, it was 'Line up your shoes; go take a bath.' With grandkids, it's different. He's had more fun with them. He goes to their sports events. At this point in his life he doesn't care if he shows his softer side."

Wow! Even old persnickety Tom Coughlin, the king of the growl, as Witz put it, has become Mr. Conviviality. And, Judy says, that connection with his grandchildren has made him better at his job. But grandchildren can't solve everything. The last game I saw, Coughlin was still scowling, still pacing back and forth and screaming his head off.

For a grandchild, having Pops in his or her life brings nothing but benefits, and I'm not talking about economic support, though, as we've seen, that may be necessary. Researchers have found that grandchildren who have a close relationship with a grandfather are likely to perform well in school, display positive emotional adjustment, have higher self-esteem and a greater ability to develop and maintain friendships.

Some grandfathers talk candidly about investing time so their grandchildren will take care of them later on. But more often they talk about how the relationship adds meaning to their lives. They experience a grandchild's unconditional love, the gratifying sense of family. Playing with children again is rejuvenating. There's a sense of personal triumph when grandchildren master a skill Grampa taught them; it's fulfilling to help shape another generation. Then there's the joy of looking at adorable little

Willie and thinking, That's me. That's me living on. Pretty powerful stuff.

A month before he died Bob Simon told me: "Aside from the great artist who knows he's a great artist, what do we have to leave behind?"

"The passing of the seed," I said.

"Exactly. Exactly. And it's totally conscious. Jack is what I'm leaving behind."

SEVEN

Step-Grandmothers

Step-grandmothers are one of the fastest growing demographics in the Western world, making up one-third of women sixty-five and over.

When I lived in Washington, I joined a women reporters' lunch group, formed in the mid-1970s when it was still hard to find many of us in newsrooms. To fit in, we would pretend to care about the 'Skins game on Sunday, and we faux-laughed at raunchy jokes (even told a few ourselves). We were thirsty for girl talk: What's a good mascara that doesn't run? Where do you get your hair done? We were suffering from the comfort-of-female-company deficiency.

There were eight of us and we met religiously, once a month. It made me see that female friendship is a real biological need, up there with air and love. It must be atavistic, going back to the Stone Age, when women spent their days together, talking in a circle.

When I moved to New York I helped form another ladies' lunch group that has met once a month for more than twenty years now, to discuss politics, investing and the best mascara. The five of us have lived through the arcs of one another's lives: through husband issues, children's romances—and breakups, boss crises, one death and the birth of grandchildren. Three of the five are step-grandmothers. Turns out our little group is a microcosm of the country, which is in the midst of a step-grandmother boom.

This is newsworthy: there are now more stepfamilies in the United States than first families, which, it would seem, puts step-grans at the heart of the New American Family. You can see it on Grandparents' Day at your local kindergarten, where it's not unusual for a child to arrive with a posse of grannies and grampas, sometimes as many as eight.

What the women in the lunch group have taught me is that despite a reputation for apple poisoning and other dastardly acts of evil (think Snow White and Cinderella), step-grandmothers (often stepmothers first) very often love the children every bit as much as biological grans do. This seems to be especially true for women who never had children of their own, like Diane Sawyer. When she told the group about the births of her step-grandchildren—four girls and a boy—she described that same apocalypse of loving that I had felt, and the same palpable attachment. I have seen Diane romping around, chasing after the little ones, making funny faces—acting just as goofy as the rest of us grans.

When Joan Ganz Cooney's step-granddaughter, Chloe, was born, she told us, "I feel reborn." Joan created and ran *Sesame Street* and the Children's Television Workshop for twenty years, so in a way, she's the mother of several generations, even while she never had a child of her own. When Chloe came along, Joan, at age sixty-seven, was seized by that deep-rooted urge to grandmother. It's like a middle-aged woman's biological clock.

"I bonded with Chloe right away. It was magic, a new kind of head-over-heels love," she told me. She even experienced the grandparent's blind bedazzlement: "I thought she was the most beautiful thing I'd ever seen. A year later when I looked at her pictures, she was covered with red wine stains from the forceps." Joan shakes her head, laughing. "She doesn't even look normal. Her hair stood on end like Don King's."

"You never saw it," I said knowingly.

"All I saw was the most gorgeous baby I had ever seen, and she was mine."

Even women with a loose connection to a baby can feel that welling-up. Feminist Germaine Greer, author of *The Female Eunuch* (1970) and one of the major voices for women's liberation, has told the story of her caring for the infant daughter of a friend. "Ruby lit up my life in a way that nobody, certainly no lover, ever has done. I was not prepared for the incandescent sensuousness of this small child, the generosity of her innocent love."

Sure enough, when I looked into it, there is evidence that *unrelated* women can experience some of the same biochemical changes in reaction to a baby as mothers who go through childbirth. A study on foster mothers showed "a significant oxytocin production in response to a cuddle interaction."

If this can happen with a foster mother and Germaine Greer, then surely it does with a step-gran. And once that body-soul connection is made with a baby, it embeds. It seeps throughout. The thought of losing that child—of being deprived of its touch—can be unbearable. I was told about a case in Israel of a mother—I'll call her Tzipi (I like the name)—who was so appalled that her daughter was a lesbian, she disowned her. But things changed when her daughter's girlfriend had a baby, a little girl. Slowly, Tzipi found a way to forgive and began babysitting. In a couple of years, however, her daughter broke up with the baby's mother. But by then Tzipi was so deeply attached that while her daughter left, she couldn't imagine living without that little girl. She had become the complete grandmother. She wouldn't give that up for anything.

When you delve into the science of all this, you come upon things you never imagined. I talked to Harvard biology professor Katie Hinde via Skype. She's an expert on lactation. In many cultures around the world, she told me, babies get milk from somebody other than their mothers. In this country, she said, adoptive mothers breast-feed.

"Really? I've never heard of that."

"That's pretty common, and," she added, "grandmothers also breast-feed."

"Seriously?"

"Oh yes. In subsistence populations a grandmother could be in her thirties and still reproducing. That she lactates is not a surprise. But there have been cases where *postmenopausal* grandmothers have breast-fed."

I was astonished.

"You have to realize," she said, "that their milk is low in protein and fat, so not sufficiently nourishing." She explained that while the quality of grandmother milk is poor, her nipple can still calm a baby. She smiled. "We have pacifiers and binkies. There are cultures that call on grandmothers, both maternal and paternal, to quiet a baby." And step-grans as well.

"So is this grandmother breast-feeding going on in Western societies today?" I asked.

"Not with postmenopausal grandmothers," she said, "because" —listen to this—"they might not ever think to try."

Food for thought, so to speak.

While step-grandmothers fall for the babies, the parents of the babies rarely make it easy. Seldom is there a welcome mat. Step-grans are made to feel "less than," the odd grandparent out. These women are certainly not celebrated or honored. There's no such thing as Step-Grandmother's Day or a Hallmark card from "your loving step-grandmother." Actually there is a Stepmother's Day, the Sunday after Mother's Day—an afterthought that can feel like salt in the wound.

"Steps will tell you themselves, 'I don't know how I'm supposed to act,'" says Wednesday Martin, author of *Stepmonster* and *Primates of Park Avenue*. "They say, 'I don't know how I'm supposed to feel. I don't know what to do.' For steps, it's like driving around New York with a map of Boston. It's never easy."

Wednesday, who has interviewed scores of step-grandparents, told me, "There's a lot of societal pressure on these women—both stepmoms and step-grans—because they're supposed to be able to make this work. They're ashamed if they can't." Yet they have no etiquette book or Rand McNally to consult, no rules of the road for situations like:

- You're only thirty-five and you don't want the beloved grandson of your much-older husband calling you "Granny."
- You never had your own kids and desperately want to be a real grandmother, but the biological gran blames you for breaking up her marriage.
- Even worse, you simply can't stand the little monster.

One example of how touchy this can be is perhaps the most famous step-grandmother in the world, Camilla, the Duchess of Cornwall, wife of Prince Charles. Poor Camilla. She not only has the other grandmother, Carole Middleton, to reckon with, she has the ghost of Diana. What an irony that Diana thought of her as the "third person" in her marriage; now Camilla has Diana as the "third grandmother."

Camilla is a devoted, veteran babysitter for her own five grandchildren, but just how involved she's allowed to be with Kate and William's royal infants depends on which of the tabloids you read. One blares that it's a catfight: Camilla, the finishing school debutante, vs. Carole, the miner's daughter. Another says Camilla is Kate's confidante, knitted intrinsically into the family because she's made Papa Charles so happy. Whichever, she certainly has gotten a taste of how difficult it is for children, no matter how old they are, to accept a stepmother.

One reason is that after a divorce women usually experience

more resentment than men. What often happens is that stepchildren absorb their mother's anger and become her proxy. "In hating the stepmom," says Wednesday Martin, "a stepchild is expressing solidarity with his or her mother. If the mother gives her permission to like her stepmother, the behavior likely abates."

So, if you marry someone divorced with kids and their mother is alive, chances are you will have to run through an initiation gauntlet, a pledge week that could go on for years. When my friend Joan Cooney married Pete Peterson, the former secretary of commerce and chairman of Blackstone, he had joint custody of his five children. So overnight Joan went from the peace of no children to the hubbub of an army. And off to war they went—against Joan. Generally speaking, they tormented her.

Holly, the only girl, was fifteen. She told me that she and her brothers would do things just to rattle Joan, like leaving wet towels everywhere, knowing it would drive her crazy. "I was really tough on her," said Holly with a sheepish smile.

By the time Holly had her first child, Chloe, though, she and Joan had become friends, and then best friends. Today both women laugh about the victimization. If that's what it took to get that baby, says Joan, all is forgiven.

"Joan was at my house all the time," said Holly. "She would ask me when I was leaving for work and then sneak over to feed Chloe." Joan was running *Sesame Street* at the time and would leave the office in the middle of the day just to hold her. "She would call me at eight in the morning," said Holly, "and ask about the feeding schedule. She wanted to do it, and I was totally fine with it. It allowed me to spend a little more time at the office or to run errands. And when I traveled for work"—she was a producer at ABC News—"I always had someone I trusted to leave my child with." So Joan was encouraged to become as indulgent and doting as she wanted to be.

Not all step-grans have baby lust like Joan's. Some want no part of it. They're simply not interested. And this creates its own problems. What happens when everyone in the family is ecstatic about the coming birth except you? Or you *were* excited, but now that the little one is here, you're not that crazy about him? It happens.

I had a CBS colleague who married an older man. Now they have two children roughly the same age as her step-grandchildren, who often come to her house to play. Here's what she confided: When *her* children scream and yell and bounce off the furniture, she goes with the flow. But when the step-grandchildren scream and yell and bounce off the furniture, she feels like her skin is boiling in acid. And of course, she can never admit that to her husband. It's impossible for a step-grandmother to tell her husband that she can't stand his grandson, the apple of his eye. Or that she doesn't like being a step-gran.

Suppose a step-grandmother loves the baby but also loves her job selling real estate, or being a doctor, or teaching algebra to ninth graders. Young parents in need of help can grow to resent Step-Grandma for not being sufficiently attentive. What if the step-gran has her own grandchildren? If she's going to take young kids for the weekend or away on vacation, she'd rather they be her biological grandkids. Imagine the *tsuris* in that situation.

And a new baby can open old wounds. "Even if the biological grandmother initiated the divorce," said Wednesday Martin, "even if she's been happy, the baby kindles a new jealousy, a bitterness: 'How dare "that witch" tread on my territory. This is *my* grandson.'"

A lot's been said about ex-wives making life difficult for new wives. One of Aaron's best friends, Tom Bartholomew, beseeched me, "Don't forget us men. It's really hard for a grandfather who's divorced from Grandma." If an ex-husband is cut off from his grandchildren, he's just as agonized as Grandma.

There are times when grown children do everything they can to keep their fathers from remarrying in the first place. Often money is at stake. There's no ignoring the specter of disinheritance. Will the second wife dilute the grandchildren's birthright? I know someone who tried to sabotage her wealthy, aging father's love affair—from accusing the girlfriend of gold-digging to suggesting to her dad that falling in love at eighty-five was undignified and ridiculous: "Your friends are laughing at you." Maybe he wasn't fit to be with his grandchildren. In that case, the daughter prevailed: her father did not remarry.

When dads do remarry, the consequences can be formidable. Kings have lost their realms, CEOs have lost their companies, regular Joes their children, and everyone in the family can get swept into situations both daunting and awkward.

For instance: a young woman falls for and marries her college roommate's father. It's not that uncommon that one twenty-five-year-old becomes another twenty-five-year-old's stepmom. Awkward.

Another case is that of Linda Fairstein, a prosecutor who ran the sex crimes unit at the DA's office in New York City for thirty years and now writes bestselling crime novels. She fell in love with a young colleague's father, Justin Feldman, a lawyer twenty-eight years older. When it was announced that Linda and Justin were to marry, his daughter Jane, who actually worked for Linda in the DA's office, became the butt of merciless teasing. It didn't help when a judge asked her, "What are you getting Linda for Mother's Day?" To make matters worse, Jane's mother was not, shall we say, pleased with the new, much younger wife.

When Jane married and gave birth to a baby boy, Justin was overjoyed at becoming a grandfather. Linda was only in her early forties, but never having had her own children, she too was jubilant. That clock had been ticktocking away. A thirst in her was being slaked.

"Justin handed the baby to me and I was gone. I was in love. It was every bit like holding my own flesh and blood. And I loved seeing Justin that happy."

Twenty months later, a second grandson arrived, and it happened all over again. "I held them both from the time they were born," Linda said. "I wasn't going to be a grandmother any other way. And I wanted to be in the grandmother role. I didn't want the 'step' to be any part of it."

"Why?" I asked. "Because of the stigma of step?"

"No. It was so important to Justin. He watched to see how and whether I bonded with these kids."

"For someone to have a good relationship with a stepmother," says Wednesday Martin, "his or her mother has to 'release' them from the 'loyalty bind.' It doesn't happen that often. It's easier if the biological gran has remarried or partnered." Neither of which was the case with Justin's ex.

So there was work to do. Justin made it clear that he and Linda were a unit; they had to be accepted as a pair of grandparents. As it was, Linda was so genuinely eager to be involved, it cemented the marriage and eventually wore Jane down. How could she rebuff someone who was so rhapsodic about her children?

"I wanted this badly," Linda told me. "I wanted it to work." She was so intent, she launched a research project on how she should comport herself. The wisest advice was from her friend Catherine: "You're the third grandmother. You just be Auntie Mame."

Next issue: what would she be called? "I wanted to be Granny Linny," Linda told me. Most of the steps I spoke to, afraid to offend, shy away from "Granny" anything. But this is what Linda insisted on. And yet, when one of the grandsons began to talk, he refused to say it. "I would take the boys to a bakery and say: 'You can't have a cinnamon bun'—their favorite—'unless you call me Granny Linny.' And still the older boy wouldn't. He'd just roll his eyes. I even made Justin take him for a walk and lean on him. But he said: 'That's ridiculous. She's too young to be my grandma.'" He called her Linda.

When Justin died, it became Linda's primary mission to maintain the relationships. A couple of years later, when she decided to remarry, the boys' reactions were the only ones she cared about. "My biggest fear," she said, "was that my bond with them might be loosened." She asked them to fly to New York to meet her fiancé. It was role reversal: now she was the one who needed *him* to bond with *her* grandchildren. The boys gave the okay; they wanted her to be happy. It was like getting FDA approval.

"Now you're their only grandmother," I said. Justin's first wife had died as well.

"I'm their only. I'm the granny."

The world of step-grans is a minefield. Everyone should tread gingerly, requests carefully thought out. For instance, a father might ask his son or daughter if his new wife can be called "Grandma." What if the answer is no? What kind of ill will follows that?

When you go to the advice blogs, you're told not to be insistent about a title. Pick something neutral, or a Disneyfied version of your own name, like NeeNee or Pookie. Once you decide on a name, everyone starts calling you BeeBee or Nonna. All that awkwardness over how your son-in-law or daughter-in-law addresses you—first name, Mom, Dad, Mrs. or Mr.—goes away. In my case, even my niece and nephew call me Lolly now. My own daughter calls me Lolly and it's okay by me.

But it isn't only what the baby calls the step-gran that causes grief; it can be what she calls herself. Wednesday told me about a successful, high-functioning "nice guy" whose mother had died five years before. His stepmother never made the mistake of saying, "Call me Mommy." But then he heard her refer to herself as his son's "grandmother"—and he snapped. He picked up the baby and stomped off. He said, "It felt like a slap in my mother's face. This was my mother's name."

Perhaps the prickliest of all is what happens when a young wife gets along better with her husband's stepmother than with his biological mom, her mother-in-law. As one young mother explained: "It's like having a mother-in-law without all the bullshit." Her husband's mother manages to alienate even long-distance, sending overbearing e-mails in which she conveys a disdain for the way the new wife is raising her son. "Each message is drenched with disapproval of how the baby was dressed or fed or disciplined," said the young woman. I could feel her tense up. "It's so hard to turn the other cheek, to sit on my anger when she's on my case. It's *our* baby and we'll raise him the way *we* want to. With my stepmother-in-law, the relationship is so much easier."

I found myself feeling sorry for the biological gran. "She's suffering, I assure you," I told the young mother. "I'll bet she has no idea she's being critical."

What's even worse than having a daughter-in-law who prefers the step-gran is having a grandchild who likes the step more.

What I learned in my interviews is that for every grandmother story of unalloyed fulfillment, there's one of suffering, especially for the steps. Many of them fall into the trap of trying too hard, which is often read as "interfering." One woman I interviewed, Mrs. X, sounded perplexed. "I can't open my mouth. One little word of helpful advice and he [her stepson] acts like I've committed a crime. I'm told, 'You can't treat my wife that way.' I don't even know what I did. It's all too much."

Mrs. X asked me not to use her name as she confided her chagrin. She loves the baby, her first grandchild, but has been made to feel "once removed, looking in through a pane of glass." She complained about her stepson: "He keeps me at bay. And he distorts everything I say. It's like Hezbollah's disinformation campaign!"

I told her about a poll of stepmothers I'd seen: two-thirds said, "I would never have married this man with children, if I knew what I know now."

"Me too," she said. "I agree. I would never have done it."

She said she has volunteered to babysit, but they never take her up on it. "After a while, you give up trying and withdraw. It's a matter of self-protection." Now Mrs. X has developed her own resentments. She sees her son-in-law's generation of parents as overly absorbed in child-rearing. "They've become tedious. It's different from our generation, right? They are big-time into it, and I find it A, boring, and B, peculiar."

She said she speaks for lots of grandmothers who feel the same. "We adored our children, but they were an adjunct, a part of our lives. It wasn't all baby, all the time. If we knew how this generation was going to function with their kids, we would've been embarrassed." In case I didn't get the point, she added: "It's boring. It's boring, it's boring. There's no other conversation."

Time magazine ran a cover story in October 2015 echoing Mrs. X's observation that millennials are obsessed with parenting, under pressure to be attentive in a way the baby boomers weren't. *Time* cited a recent survey showing that 80 percent of young mothers say it's important to be "the perfect mom," compared with 64 percent of all mothers.

Taylor and Andrew are relatively relaxed parents, but they have not escaped their generation's zeal when it comes to the rights and wrongs. One right is breast-feeding, now considered de rigueur. It's close to a moral imperative. Oh, the shame if a mom doesn't conform.

It hit home for me when Tay went back to work, and had to

pump. She dragged that contraption around—with those Valkyrian cups and the rest of the paraphernalia—wherever she went, submitting to the daily unpleasantness of a machine clamped to her breasts as if they were udders. A part of me rejoiced when the *New York Times* ran an article called "Overselling Breast-Feeding," questioning whether it actually provides all the benefits it's said to, and suggesting that the breast-pump industry is pumping the hype.

I don't want to sound defensive about the way my friends and I raised our kids. But, as I've said under my breath many a time, "We didn't do *that* and you turned out great."

Getting back to Mrs. X, her stepson's rejection of her seems self-defeating. He and his wife could use her help; they need babysitters and she wouldn't charge them a penny. Some adult children are wise enough to embrace the step-grandmother as a way of giving their children grounding in a big family. What this stepson is doing is depriving his child, who, like all children, can never have too many people who love them.

A lot of the advice for step-grans amounts to: don't expect too much and "lean back," not in—let the children and their parents come to you. But here's why this role is so damn hard. If you lean too far back, it'll probably be translated as indifference. So while you're leaning back, you need to convey how wonderful, perfect and lovable you think the child is.

As for the parents of the babies: Be the grown-ups. Get over it, your parents' divorce. And put what's best for your child first.

None of this comes naturally, of course. It has to be a conscious project, an example of which I witnessed firsthand when I visited one of my friends, whom I found in baggy pants, galoomping after her flock of step-grandchildren. Actually, she was number six in a phalanx of adults doing the I'm-gonna-get-yous: two sets of parents, my friend the step-gran and one more—the biological grandmother. She was in the thick of it, and not for just the day, or even the week. She lived right next door.

What happened was that my friend and the ex-wife agreed they had to find a way to take the pressure off the kids. So they came to an accommodation "for the sake of the children." Soon they were all together for holidays, then vacations, and now they live side by side over the summers.

"Why even write about steps?" asked the father of two of the children. "We don't draw a distinction. There's no difference for us or the kids."

"But one day," my friend interrupted, "they'll realize I'm not their biological grandmother."

"No, no," said her stepson emphatically. "You're their grandmother, and that'll never change." Looking over at me, he added, "This is our family. These are our children's grandfather and grammas."

Later in the afternoon, I told my friend and her husband that I had never seen anything like it: a grandma and step-grandma in such comfortable harmony.

"Oh," said my friend, "it's more and more common."

She may be right.

Jennie Held, one of the producers at *60 Minutes*, is beautiful, with such a big, open smile, she compels you to warm to her. I assumed that her ability to raise two children and keep her job with total equilibrium was a function of her sunny temperament. It was. But that's only part of the reason.

Jennie married an Austrian-born musician named Stefan Held. Their two young children, Juliet and Mateo, have four grandmothers, like a lot of their friends. Two live in Austria; Jennie's mom and stepmom live nearby in New York.

Even though Jennie's parents were divorced twenty years ago, there was no love lost between those two women. But that changed once Juliet was born and Jennie needed help. She and Stefan both travel and work late nights, Jennie at *60 Minutes*, Stefan at his gigs. And they can't afford full-time child care. Cue the grammas.

"I couldn't do it without them. I certainly couldn't keep working," Jennie told me. She showed me the babysitting schedule: Mondays, stepmom; Tuesdays, a babysitter; Wednesdays and Thursdays, her mom; Fridays it's her mom again with a babysitter.

The great thaw between the grandmothers started with their calling each other to swap days. The reschedulings turned into chats, then sharing stories, then confiding. Now they even babysit *together*.

"If you're a biological grandmother," said Jennie, "you put your kids and grandkids in an awful position if you won't deal with the new wife. We used to have separate birthday parties, two Christmases, et cetera. We would always be choosing, always forced to cut someone out."

Now everyone is together for all birthdays and holidays. Jennie tells me with her dazzling smile, "Now it's no surprise to find my mother's boyfriend chatting with my stepmother about the kids—when they babysit together."

As I've said, Grandparents' Day at school can be an exercise in havoc. Wednesday Martin said that at her son's preschool, things got pretty confusing. "What if granny's partner is a woman? Are they Gramma and Grampa? Or what about Gramma and her boyfriend? Or Grampa and *his* boyfriend?" The school threw in the towel and decided to call it "Special Grown-ups' Day."

Divorce and remarriage create endless confusion. Things can become radioactive when new parents have to go on a round of grandparent visits: the wife's dad, then her mom, and then his dad and partner . . . and his mom. Four places with two children. Not seeing them all is its own trip to perdition.

Songstress Katie Goodman (Ellen's daughter) and her husband, Soren Kisiel, wrote and have performed a song called "The Easter Bunny Can Only Come Once." Here are some of the lyrics, about four sets of grandparents scattered all over the country:

Your grandparents in California still find a few of last year's eggs hidden about
But since Easter overlaps with Passover this time, looks like the Jews lucked out.
Having eight grandparents is the best you can get. Four houses with four different Lego sets.
One grampa who can teach you how to skin a deer, another how to make crepe suzettes.
Having eight grandparents isn't usually par for the course
But who says good things don't come out of divorce!

EIGHT

Hope Meadows: A Road Trip

My granddaughter came to spend a few weeks with me, and I decided to teach her to sew. After I had gone through a lengthy explanation of how to thread the machine, she stepped back, put her hands on her hips, and said in disbelief: "You mean you can do all that, but you can't play my Game Boy?"

—AUTHOR UNKNOWN

It's unseemly to gush, especially for a reporter. We're supposed to stand coolly on the sidelines, keeping our opinions to ourselves and our emotions holstered, analyzing the facts with balanced sobriety. Well, screw that when it comes to the story of Hope Meadows.

Hope is an extraordinary place. It's a planned community in Rantoul, Illinois, created for the sole purpose of rescuing children who were abused, neglected or abandoned. This amazing community plucks these kids out of the foster care system, where they have often been discarded by one family after the next. At Hope Meadows they are adopted into stable homes in a lovely, safe neighborhood. And here's the secret sauce: the neighborhood comes with grandparents.

A group of retired senior citizens—some feeling they too had been discarded—have moved there to help heal the children. But—and this was not foreseen—the children end up healing them.

When I went to visit, I was told, "This is no Utopia," but by my lights, it's as close as it gets. I arrived in September 2014 to find a small village of look-alike ranch houses with well-tended lawns. Kids were everywhere, climbing trees, playing in the streets and buzzing around on their bikes. Except for the skateboards, it's a throwback to the Eisenhower years—with one other exception: most of the children are minorities and most of the adults are white.

The story of Hope started over twenty years ago when Dr. Brenda Krause Eheart, a professor of child development, was studying the foster care system in Illinois. What she found was distressing, particularly one case that just stuck in her craw. She was at the Department of Children and Family Services when a set of foster parents called and announced, "We can't parent Johnny anymore."

Brenda is trim and stylish, with short, graying hair. When I first met her, she bounded toward me, introduced herself and added, "I'm seventy and a grandmother!" She's her own electromagnetic field radiating vitality.

"Johnny had been picked up at school by a social worker he didn't know and a policeman he didn't know." As Brenda tells me the story, her voice deepens with outrage. "My gosh, he's eight years old." Her hands are twitching. "I just couldn't stand it. I had to do something."

She knew from her study that many foster parents eventually give up on the children. She wondered: if a group of those parents lived together in something like a compound, wouldn't they help each other persevere? So she went in pursuit of housing for an experiment. "It had to be a place where I would raise my own kids," she said.

Eventually, her search took her to Chanute Air Force Base in Rantoul, near the University of Illinois, which was being closed. The minute she saw the residential quarters, she wanted them. This place was perfect. She could see living there herself. Only one thing would stand in her way: the Pentagon bureaucracy. "Thank goodness," she admitted, "I'm one pushy lady." Two years and two thousand phone calls later she got her nice neighborhood.

Chanute was the largest air force training base in the country, with hundreds of well-built attached duplexes for married airmen. All Brenda needed was twelve. What they offered her was a twenty-two-acre subdivision of eighty houses, take it or leave it. She had raised enough money (partly with a million-dollar grant from the state of Illinois) and was tired of arguing, so she bought all eighty for $225,000 and set about populating her hamlet. After screening the potential parents, she matched them up with three or four children. That's because many of the kids were taken from their abusive homes along with their brothers and sisters. Brenda felt it was important to keep siblings together.

Most of the original group of parents were married white couples, though there were some African-Americans and some single women. If they accepted several kids, they were given for free a six- or seven-bedroom house, created by combining two duplex units. If a parent stayed home to care for the children, he or she was considered an "employee," which meant they got a salary of $19,000 a year plus health benefits.

But what about the grandparents? "It was serendipitous, a total fluke," Brenda told me. The idea began when a friend was telling her about people who were retiring and needed to downsize because they could no longer afford their big houses. Brenda had an epiphany: why not offer retirees the smaller three-bedroom duplexes for $525 a month, in exchange for six hours a week of volunteer work? Her motive was simply to fill her extra forty-eight houses.

The seniors' becoming "grandparents" happened organically, without design. Because their houses were scattered in among the children's—next door or across the street—they saw each other all the time. As Brenda explained: "The seniors immediately got to know the children, and then how do you not fall in love?"

One thing that seemed to facilitate the introductions was that each of the houses had an attached carport, where the seniors liked to sit on lawn chairs. Because there were no steps, no barriers (and usually no cars), kids would walk or ride their bikes right into the carports and start talking. And in the process, they began re-creating the extended family. That's what's most striking about Hope: that these total strangers of different races, creeds and circumstances came together and fused into the multigenerational families of old.

One of the parents, Kenny Calhoun, told me: "It reminds me of where I grew up in South Frankfort, Kentucky. It was a small community, and the grandparents, they would be outdoors in their chairs, watching over us. Everybody knew everybody. And believe me, it works."

Irene Bohn, a retired schoolteacher and one of the most popular grandmothers at Hope Meadows, was the queen of the carports. She was out there on her swing most every day: "You sit here and you watch the children and you think, Where would that child be if they weren't here in this place?" Irene reflected. "And where would I be? Probably vegetating someplace, if I were even still on this earth. I don't know. It's just so beautiful to see the little kids come here and often do a complete turnaround."

I was in her spotless living room, surrounded by photos of her Hope Meadows grandchildren, past and present—dozens of them. Irene has short, curly gray hair and kind eyes behind her oval-shaped glasses. She was wearing Bermuda shorts and dangling earrings that seemed in keeping with her spunk, even now at ninety. She's one of many examples there of how being a surrogate granny is good for one's health.

Irene was among the first seniors to move to Hope Meadows, so she's had many opportunities to help the children. "I really thought when I taught school that I knew it all. I didn't know anything. Not when you hold a crack baby in your arms, or meet a little boy six years old who didn't even know how to use a crayon. He had never seen one." She sighed. "Oh, I shed many a tear." Irene gazed off to inhabit that memory. "I'll tell you the thing that really gets me. You look into their eyes. And—and you see hunger. You see 'Don't hit me.'" I felt chills, thinking how fortunate my daughter and granddaughter are.

The foster children who come to Hope are often the toughest ones in the system, the kids with attachment disorders and explosive anger. Many contend with serious medical problems, having been physically abused or exposed to drugs in utero.

Irene likes to order pizza, sit with a kid on her lap and watch movies. It's one reason she's so popular. Another is because she tells the children, as she told me, what happened to her when she was a little girl: "I was a nun for over thirty years. But it was my dad's decision, it wasn't mine." Her father forced her into a convent in Joliet, Illinois, when she was just thirteen. She clenched her fists and scowled. "He put me there, and I still cry about it," as she cried in the bathtub every night at the convent. "I wanted to be home. I always wanted to be home." She tells the children she knows what it's like to live with pain for years on end.

When Irene finally left the convent, she taught in a public school, fell in love and married the school superintendent. When he died thirteen years later, she moved to Hope Meadows.

One of her first "grandchildren" was Brandon Laws, who had been physically abused in foster care. He's the little boy who had never held a crayon. Irene became his life raft. She is so good-natured and agreeable, so nonjudgmental and openhearted, that Brandon warmed to her. She would sit patiently and listen to him, and smother him with grandmother hugs. And she often took him with her when she went to visit her family's farm. On their first car ride there, he told her he was afraid her relatives wouldn't like him because he was black. But the minute they arrived, one of Irene's brothers lifted Brandon up onto a huge combine and let him drive. Ice broken, Brandon became a regular at the farm. By then he was calling her Grandma.

Irene tutored Brandon after school, along with his brothers Charlie and Angelo. She's one of the many seniors who help the kids get through school, which explains why 90 percent of the adopted kids have graduated from high school or earned an equivalent certificate, as compared with only 30 percent in foster care.

The children come to Hope unmoored, often angry and untrusting, yet still thirsty for attention, like Marty Calhoun, another little boy Irene tutored.

"He called you Grandma, too?" I asked.

"Uh-huh. Marty said, 'Grandma, do you live alone? You shouldn't ever live alone.' And I looked into his eyes. I couldn't help it, but the tears rolled down my face. He looked up at me, his little face, it just pleaded, 'Love me. Love me.' And I did. I did."

I asked her if all the children are transformed.

"You can't save them all, honey. For most we work wonders. But every once in a while, the old serpent shows its head again and the kid falls back. What they've been through, it's indelible, it's impressed on that little guy's heart."

By the time the children come here, most of them have metabolized the toxicity of their upbringing. They're prisoners of their hurt and rage. The people of Hope are trying to break open the cell doors with acts of durable, persistent affection. Kids are like kites. They need someone down there they can trust at the other end of the string.

Two of Irene's fellow grandparents from the early years at Hope, George King and Eddie Foster, devoted themselves to a boy named Alexander. He had a temper so volatile, outbursts so ferocious, that he was considered a threat to the other children. But the two grandfathers went to work. To help Alexander stay in school, they took turns accompanying him to his classes and to the lunchroom. They would sit next to him to keep him from being disruptive. I began to equate all the children at Hope Meadows, all the Alexanders, with wounded warriors suffering from PTSD. They arrive in a state of fearful embattlement, constantly reliving the terrors of their childhood traumas.

"There have been times when I thought, Why did I come here?" Irene said. "But I know why. On account of the children." Often people her age are lonely, isolated and bored. Not her. Not only does she have friends her own age, she has a purpose—a noble purpose. Irene believes these twenty years have been her happiest. "You can put your head on the pillow at night and say, 'You know, I did help someone today.'"

Surrogate grandparents are much like garden-variety grans. They buy presents, take the little ones on fun outings and defy the rules by sneaking them candy bars and ice cream.

But they don't always start out that way. Take Anita Hochberger, now seventy-five. It was her husband, Maury, who was drawn to Hope by the low rent and safe streets. When it came to that six hours of volunteer work, Anita told her husband that she would be willing to work in the office, but said, "I will not work with the children."

When I met Anita, she was wearing a bright, colorful sweater and tended to exaggerate embarrassment and surprise—embarrassment that everyone seemed to love her, and surprise that she'd ended up there.

"I had no intention of ever working with the kids," she told me.

"Do you have your own children?"

"No."

"And never wanted kids?"

Anita shakes her head firmly. "Never." When Maury moved to Hope, Anita was still working as a travel agent in Chicago, so she commuted on weekends. She was bemused when she'd show up and find any number of kids in the house, acting as if they were at home, calling Maury Grandpa. "He was very close with them. I'd never seen him like that before."

Anita moved to Hope full-time thirteen years ago, after Maury died. "I don't take to little kids," she explained. "I just don't feel comfortable with them, especially boys under first grade."

So how did she go from "I won't deal with the kids" to being one of the most active grandmothers in the compound? Well, after Maury's death, the children kept coming to her house, maybe because she kept up his habit of serving them ice cream.

The turning point came when a young boy dropped some of his ice cream on the floor. "We both looked down and I just continued my conversation with him," said Anita. "I can still see the look of relief on his face that I didn't yell at him. So that kind of started it." She smooths her perfectly coiffed hair, and her eyes crinkle up. "Another time I stupidly said to him, 'Oh, if you ever need help with homework, just come over here.'" She laughs. "What was I thinking? It was stupid to say 'cause I can't help anyone with their homework. It's so over my head!"

But he ended up being the first of many who stopped by after school for help. One of the mothers told me that when she moved in, Miss Anita told her, "I can't spend much time with your kids. I'm already a grandmother, I already have kids I do stuff with." Now, the mother told me, Anita's the one who spends the most time with her children. She takes them and other kids out to restaurants when one of them has a birthday; she takes small groups of kids on trips to Chicago to go to museums and shop.

Anita Hochberger is not lonely, she's not isolated, she's not bored. She is getting back as much as she's giving in this life that her late husband, Maury, chose for her.

I used to think life had four necessities: food, oxygen, love and friendship. Now I know there's a fifth: purpose.

For the seniors at Hope Meadows, the purpose isn't only sustaining the children. They are also anchoring and assisting the adoptive parents, who, for the most part, have taken on more than they can handle by themselves.

The parents who come to Hope are carefully selected. They are vetted, interviewed multiple times, and given extensive training. In the beginning, in 1994, they were predominantly married couples, but today, says Brenda, most of them are well-educated single women in their thirties who didn't see a way to have a family of their own and were nervous to adopt as single mothers.

Listening to Whitney Gossett's story, I realized the genius of the grandparent brigades. When I met her, I thought she looked like the girl in Renoir's *Bal du Moulin de la Galette,* except Whitney had a perpetual expression of being under siege. And I guess she was.

Whitney Gossett with her children Jeremiah, 7, Andrew, 12, Patrick, 13, and Bella, 10, along with her fiancé, Brad Burtcher.

In 2009 Whitney went from being alone to, in one whiplash of a day, being the mother of four troubled children. "I went from single, living in a duplex, driving a VW Bug, to four children all at once, driving a minivan," she laughs, telling me her story. She adopted four siblings—well, four with the same mother—with wretched histories of abuse and neglect. "The first six months I was crazy. Crazy because the kids were yellin' and screamin' and jumpin' all over the place." She leaned in, hoping to make me understand. "I'm not going to sit here and lie; it makes you want to hurt them sometimes. You really have to control your temper, because you want to, you know, smack the mouth or smack the butt or something."

It's been five years and she still has her days. Ah, I thought, the dark secret of motherhood: the get-me-out-of-here impulse that even the most exemplary of mothers have from time to time and are ashamed to admit. But come on, who hasn't wanted to slam the door and leave for good?

Poor Whitney had it fourfold. "It's hard when you're by yourself and they're all acting up at once. I couldn't do it without the seniors." She pauses, a hint of desperation in her eyes. "So one day I was having quite a meltdown and called one of the seniors, Carol Netterfield, and said, 'Can you just come over here?' I was at the end of my rope." She made a twisting gesture with her hands. "So Carol came over and sat with them for forty-five minutes while I just left and went off by myself."

I got the feeling that talking about this gave her a boost. She continued, "It's wonderful to know that you can pick up the phone and call somebody and they're not going to hesitate about coming over and sitting with your kids so you're not stressed out."

My God, these parents are saints. Irene Bohn, the ex-nun, says she admires them every day. "It's hard to take on someone else's child. Your blood doesn't run through them, through their veins, though later on, your love probably does. I mean, to be responsible for their lives, all the way through, and not know their background when you get them. That's a tremendous load."

Whitney didn't realize how big a load she was taking on, four kids arriving all at once: Patrick, eight; Andrew, seven; Bella, five; and the baby, Jeremiah, just shy of two, born addicted to cocaine.

"Do they at all look alike, with the same mother?" I asked.

"No way," she chuckled. Patrick's dad was white, "so he's

white-white." Andrew and Bella's dad was Hispanic, Jeremiah's African-American. She told me about some of the abuses these children had suffered. "One of my children was locked in a closet. One of 'em was made to stand in a corner while they were shooting him with an air pistol." In other words, the children have been taught that the meaning of "adult" is agony, physically and psychologically.

Whitney's kids, like all the children at Hope Meadows, can choose as many grandparents as they want. The operative word is "choose." Through trial and error, the seniors learned that the initial instinct of these bruised and battered children was to fend off adult advances. So it's best to let them make the first move. As Marty Calhoun, the boy who made Irene Bohn cry, said, "You can't rush a kid . . . You gotta just let 'em ease on in."

I was thinking there must be something hardwired in grandparents—biological, step or surrogate—that makes them unusually understanding and loving. But Whitney set me straight. "A lot of the kids here have not only been abused by parents, but they've been abused by grandparents. For the kids, sometimes the whole family is abusive. The parents learned it from their parents." What used to drive Whitney nuts when she was a caseworker in the foster care system was that the state would take the children away from neglecting parents and turn them over to neglecting or battering grandparents. It made me think: "Gramma, what big teeth you have."

"These kids got broken down by being hit and yelled at and told that they're stupid from all directions," she said. "Here they're talked to gently, and if they act up, they're told, 'Calm down, but we still love you.'"

The parents go to training classes, where they're taught how to set boundaries firmly but lovingly. Whitney had to learn how to be strict with her kids. This was not the way she was raised. "My mom sometimes looks at me and says, 'I never made *you* do that.'"

"How is your mother with these kids?" I asked.

"She loves them." It's not uncommon for these children to have both surrogate and adoptive grandparents.

The surrogates at Hope go to the training sessions too, and read the latest research, so at least everyone's on the same page. Carol Netterfield, one of the grans Whitney leans on, told me she goes to the classes to learn how to deal with children born with fetal alcohol syndrome or how to handle kids who have gone through multiple homes and are wondering, How long is *this* one going to last?

"It's just one hundred percent different than the way we raised our kids back in our generation," she said. "We used to give our kids time-outs. Now we've got a quiet corner. I'm still a little bewildered with this, but the idea is we don't send them there, they go there themselves. We say, 'Do you think maybe you need to use the quiet corner?' or, 'Would you like to just kind of get your act together?' We have to teach them to know when they're about to have a meltdown so they can self-regulate."

I was wondering what it was specifically that made Hope Meadows work so well for the children. Certainly, the grandparent factor was key, but Whitney had another answer: "Number one, there are a lot of other adopted kids in this neighborhood, so they're not alone and they don't feel different. Your mom's white and you're black, but you don't see anything different because that's the whole neighborhood. And that's another thing," she said, "there's no racial issue here whatsoever. I mean, I have not seen it and my kids haven't ever seen it either."

Many of the seniors, if not most of them, grew up in all-white communities, rarely interacting with black or Latino kids, let alone imagining that one day they would run up and call them Gramma or Grampa.

Four months after my visit, Whitney got her just reward. She met a man who came to love her children. Whitney married Brad Burtcher in September 2015. He told NPR's Ina Jaffe, "I plan on adopting all of them so they're my children. These are my kids."

One of the seniors who moved in early on was Bill Biederman. Bill had pale white skin, a paunch and wispy hair. I saw him in a photograph in which he was holding Ashley, a six-year-old black child with a ponytail. His eyes were closed as her head rested on his shoulder, both of them at peace. What special current was passing back and forth between them? Surely he was communicating that he thought she was wonderful, lovable, special, and she was telling him the same. It was like Shel Silverstein's *The Missing Piece.*

What's happened here is that all the barriers between age, race, education and income have come down. It's teamwork with a common goal. The cohesiveness is so unique that one of the mothers, Jeanette Laws, said that she instructs her adopted kids: "Now, if you go to some other town, you can't just run up to every white woman with gray hair and give her a hug and call her Grandma. They might not react like they do here."

Bill Biederman came to Hope Meadows at age fifty-seven, after several heart attacks. He had stopped working and was leading a life of disability and despondency, sitting home feeling sorry for himself. But as has happened with many of the senior men, coming to Hope Meadows and interacting with the children restored Bill's vigor and joy of living.

These men, who once wasted away in front of their television sets, are always busy, tossing a ball around with kids, planting a garden, giving after-school computer training. One of them took on the newsletter and assigned children to be the reporters.

Brenda Eheart told me about George King, one of the grandfathers who sat with Alexander in school. "He had been depressed and sour, and so frail, he had a home health nurse. We probably wouldn't have accepted him if we'd known his health was that bad," she said, showing me his photo: a black man about five foot ten with a receding hairline. He's standing in his carport smiling at six little kids playing in the sprinklers on his lawn. Brenda said that after just three months at Hope, George told the nurse not to come anymore. "He sprang back to life and lasted another fifteen years, though when he first arrived he was given less than a year." If only Ponce de León had come to Rantoul instead of Palm Beach!

The reason people here say Hope isn't paradise is because it's a real neighborhood, populated with complicated people who are black and white, highly educated and blue collar, and sometimes they get on one another's nerves. There's gossip and backstabbing like anywhere else. The parents can feel unappreciated, the seniors put-upon. And despite everyone's best intentions, not every child can be rescued. And while it's rare that seniors ever move away, roughly one family a year leaves, often in search of better schools than the ones in Rantoul.

Walking along one of the three curved streets of the village, I waved to the seniors in their carports as they were visiting with one another. It felt so safe, it reminded me of my hometown in northern Massachusetts, back when we didn't lock our doors. I was heading off to meet Carol Veit, one of the grandmothers the frazzled parents are always calling on for help.

Carol is trim and spry at seventy-one, with a puckish sense of humor. "I could be a *great*-grandmother," she tells me, which seemed impossible. She was in cargo pants looking no older than forty. She first read about Hope Meadows in the Southwest Airlines in-flight magazine in 2002, when she was a divorced mother of two, working as a pediatric physical therapist in the El Paso, Texas, school system. She thought about that article for the next eight years, until she retired in 2010 and came directly here.

I met Carol at the home of thirty-nine-year-old Diane Wheeler, one of the single moms. Diane had moved here from Michigan in June 2013 with her ten-year-old biological daughter, Danielle. Now she was in the process of adopting Kishawn, also ten. So she has two children: Danielle, blond with sparkling blue eyes, and Kishawn, African-American with dark, wary eyes.

Both Danielle and Kishawn are close to several of the seniors but closest to Carol Veit, who lives across the street. She has become an integral part of Diane's and the children's lives. So much so that Diane said, "I wouldn't be able to adopt Kishawn if Carol weren't here."

We gathered in Diane's spacious living room, Kishawn planted on a couch next to Carol. He had moved in only nine months before, and it was clear he was still getting his bearings, just learning to relax his guard. He was an elfish-looking boy who sat incredibly still for a kid his age. He was wearing a plain T-shirt and khaki pants.

Danielle, on the other hand, was in shorts and a neon T-shirt with "Hello Kitty" spelled out in glitter. Outgoing and fidgety, she never stopped moving or talking. "Temperament and T-shirt cut from the same cloth," Diane said, smiling. "If there was a rainbow of children's personalities, I have one at each end."

Explaining why she had come here, Diane said, "First off, I wanted more children, and here you have other families who are doing what you're doing. The kids have other kids who understand what they've been through. They're not the odd man out."

"Kishawn," I asked, "you get a lot of other kids here who are like you?"

"Uh-huh." His head was down. It seemed to be painful for him to say more than a few words. Diane shot him a reproachful look. "Come on," she said, "we talked about this." She was urging him to be more responsive.

"Do you like going to school?" I asked as Carol cast him a reassuring smile.

"Kinda." He and Danielle were both in fifth grade at a public elementary school in Rantoul.

Danielle began teasing Carol, who shook her head in mock dismay. It struck me that Danielle might be as important to

Kishawn's recovery as Diane and Carol. There are twelve biological children at Hope, who, like Danielle, demonstrate to their adopted siblings that grown-ups there aren't like the ones they'd known before. These kids are putting on a daily show-and-tell that says: if you reach out your hand to *these* people, it won't get slapped.

One thing I've learned about in my job is the power of a visual image. Watching television, for instance, we decide if we like or trust a politician by what we see (not so much by what they say), which is why they're always smiling. Kishawn's irrepressible sister was starring in little visual vignettes for his psychological edification.

"What are *you* getting out of Hope Meadows?" I asked Carol.

"If the kids were gone, I'd go. I'm not here for the relationship between the seniors. I just love being around kids. I get to be a kid."

"Yeah, all the kids line up outside her house," said Diane.

"I know how to play." Carol laughed. "If they're in my house, I'm in the middle of the floor with them. We play games." There was a tent up in her living room next to a toy corner stacked with board games. It looked like my living room when Jordan comes to visit.

"And Kishawn," said Diane, trying to engage her son, "you've been cooking over there, haven't you?"

"Uh-huh." He had a throw pillow up against his chest, a protective shield. But while he didn't say much, he was engaged, paying attention.

Diane is tall and thin, with a straightforward, no-nonsense manner, which is how she told me the story of Kishawn's coming to live with her. When she arrived at Hope, Kishawn was living in the house next door, along with three of his siblings. One morning she got an unexpected call asking if she could take in some children that day. It seems the family next door—without any warning—just picked up and moved out, leaving four children behind. There had been no final adoption, so apparently they were within their rights. I was told this was rare at Hope, but it happens.

Kishawn, knowing none of this, was taken out of school and brought to the Hope Meadows office, where he was introduced to Diane and told, "Here's your new mom." It was that abrupt. "He met me in the office and came home with me fifteen minutes later," said Diane. "He had no say."

God almighty. I wanted to find the family that abandoned those four kids and wallop them. But who am I to judge? Who knows how far their patience had been tested?

This was not a new experience for Kishawn, except this time he was separated from his brothers and sister. Two of them moved in with a family two houses down the street, but his favorite brother, the most unruly of the bunch, was sent away. "In my situation," explained Diane, "I felt I could take just one."

I thought: How is this different from what Brenda witnessed with little Johnny, the boy who inspired Hope Meadows in the first place? Hope was supposed to be a haven, a sanctuary, free of this kind of rejection. Then again, Kishawn now has Diane, who will be his mother for life. "It's taken Kishawn a long time to trust that," she said, "but it took no time for me to think of him as my child, and to love him the way I love Danielle."

Diane had hoped to be a stay-at-home mom, but Hope Meadows has had to change its policy. She is no longer paid a salary, nor does she receive health benefits, though she and the other parents still get a rent subsidy, which means they pay as little as $50 a month for their big houses. You couldn't live in a shoe box for that in New York—or anywhere else. Diane was looking for a full-time job. Up to then she'd worked part time. If she was ever late getting home, Danielle and Kishawn would go across the street and play with Carol.

I asked Diane if she planned to adopt any more children. She said she was thinking of fostering teenage mothers, inviting them to live with her and her kids until they were able to care for their babies on their own, which could take years.

What Diane loves at Hope is the sense of community. "When I was in the hospital for surgery, I was bombarded with visitors from the neighborhood—the other parents and the grandparents—with lists of who's taking the kids when, and who's bringing meals at what time. Everyone just pitched in and helped."

"You don't get that anywhere else," said Carol.

"I was a little surprised at how close the kids got to some of the seniors," said Diane, "and surprised at how close I feel with some of them. I have told Carol that if I move, I'm buying her a house next door, and she's coming with me."

Danielle sprang to her feet, ran to Carol and hugged her. Kishawn was no longer clutching the pillow. He was laughing with the rest of us.

Brenda Eheart did a good thing.

Too many seniors retire, voluntarily or otherwise, and find themselves living an aimless and listless life. All too often they deal with their excess leisure time by watching television more than four hours a day. People need structure in their lives. John Maynard Keynes wrote about this back in 1930. He said that society might suffer a sort of "nervous breakdown" if people have too much free time.

Hope Meadows shows that filling that time by helping youngsters is rejuvenating and replenishing. I did a *60 Minutes* profile of Ted Kennedy in 1998 when he was at the peak of his powers as the senator from Massachusetts. Little known (until our report), he was slipping out of his office one afternoon a week to go to an inner-city school in Washington to read to first graders. He was assigned to a different child each year. That year it was Jasmine Harrison, an adorable seven-year-old, who lit up when he (and I and two camera crews) showed up.

"How are you?" asked the senator, handing Jasmine a children's book about government. She smiled at him. They'd become pals.

"Here we go," he said. "You start."

Holding the picture book, Jasmine read: "America's mice have a government, too, with Presidents, Senators, and Congressmen."

The senator corrected her. "Congress what?"

"Congressmice," she said.

"Congressmice?" asked Kennedy, laughing. "That's a new word!"

He told me he did this because it was good for his soul. I was so impressed, I urged Aaron to try it. It took him a while, but starting in 2015 (yes, seventeen years later) he began volunteering at an after-school tutoring program called Page Turners. After submitting to a criminal background check, he started going to the Metro Baptist Church in Hell's Kitchen once a week to help students in grades one through eight with their homework. One week he might work on algebra with Alejandro, a sixth grader; another week he'd help Maria, a first grader, with a book report. After tutoring, he hangs around to teach a group of boys how to play chess. It reminds him of his days working on homework with Taylor, and it makes him happy. Ted Kennedy was right: helping children is good for the soul.

NINE
Chloe

It snowed last year, too. I made a snowman and my brother knocked it down and I knocked him down and then we had tea.

—DYLAN THOMAS

December 2012. Taylor and crew spent Christmas in Kansas City with Andrew's parents, while Aaron and I got our apartment ready for their visit after the holiday. On Christmas Eve we tried to assemble a kiddie stove. Who knew when I saw it online we would have to put it together ourselves? If I'd only known. There were big A screws and smaller Bs. This was Ikea for guys in Mensa. We kept attaching parts upside down or inside out, which meant unscrewing them with that effing Allen wrench. After two hours of frustration, Aaron went out to buy us a small screwdriver so we could finish. Which we did, damn proud of ourselves, even if it did take two full days.

Tay, Andrew and Jordan got to New York a few days later. One of the kicks of having a grandchild is following their metamor-

Aaron and I as guests of Jordan's tea party.

phosis from one developmental step to the next. It's like watching a Polaroid fade in. Jordan was now speaking full sentences, with proper grammar; she could count to twenty in English and ten in Spanish. I was glorying in this emerging person until I witnessed the first of many grand mal tantrums. Stomping, screaming, hot tears—and she couldn't stop. Taylor never went through this (though I've been told I did). Jordan was consumed by the tempests of the terrible twos, and for the first time ever, I saw my go-with-the-flow daughter lose it. As she dressed her, Taylor was bombarded with a hail of NOs from an insistent instrument of protest. When it reached a level of mother abuse, I had to fight off an impulse to berate the little warrior with a loud "Knock it off." Eventually, Tay had enough and she yelled, a sound so rare it sent Jordan into desperate, heaving sobs. At that point, my allegiance flipped.

We were into a running ritual of trying to soothe Jordan, all of us devoted to making her laugh. Too many times, we would give in and hand over the iPad: "You can watch Dora." That produced an instant calm, every time. As we showered her with attention, I thought: We're building her sense of worth and belief in her lovability. What a cold shower being twelve is going to be.

I had become the reading lady. I used this as a kind of a bribe, a sure way to hold my baby next to me. I would settle into a not-too-big chair and say, "Get in position," which meant up against

Making funny faces with Jordan.

me, close and tight. And then I'd read. Sometimes ten books in a sitting: *Ladybug Girl*, *Curious George*, Dora, Madeline, Olivia. I liked to get a stack so I wouldn't have to read the same one over and over.

Once during that post-Christmas vacation I babysat one whole day so Taylor and Andrew could go off by themselves. I read her a Fancy Nancy book, we drew and colored, I read her another Fancy Nancy book, then I took her out for a walk. Back home, I read the first Fancy Nancy again and got a hug. Colored some more. Read one of the Paddington Bears. "Nudder book, Lolly." This was not a request as much as a fiat. She handed me the same Fancy Nancy. I was wiped. And out of ideas to entertain her.

That's when she started whining, "I want my mommy." Then she banged her head on the headboard and sobbed for Mommy to kiss it. "No, not you, Lolly." Nothing I did assuaged her. Nothing I did was good enough. I love Jordan more than anything, but at that moment, I wanted her parents to get the hell back.

Once she did settle down, I realized there was nowhere I'd rather be. No one I'd rather be with, even when she was cranky. I would think about what Mae West once said: "Too much of a good thing—can be wonderful!"

On another babysitting day, I finally succumbed and turned on the TV. *SpongeBob SquarePants*. Phew. She would be engrossed, and I could take a breather. But Taylor called (to check up on me) and heard the TV. "Oh no!" she said with desperation. "Not *SpongeBob*. It creates ADD." Oy.

It was back to the books till I was hoarse, so I clicked on the TV again and searched for a kiddie show Tay would not kill me over.

During the following summer in Nantucket, I grabbed any chance to be with Jordan. I would drop *whatever* I was doing, gladly. I'd give up a nap or stop reading the papers. I hadn't been like that with Taylor. Back in those days I was never ever free just to simply, uncomplicatedly love my kid. Work intruded on her time, or she was intruding on my reading or my sleep. As a mother, I lived with teeth grinding and stomach turbulence from worrying about Taylor, my job, my husband's depression, the bills, my parents, Tay's piano lessons, my boss looking at me funny. My emotional neighborhood was an overcrowded tenement. I felt trapped; I was in a fight against an urge to unshackle.

There was none of that with Jordan. She is the *going to* place. The *being there* place. How rarely have I been so completely in the present? So clear of the churn about something left undone? This is the grandmother do-over. But "do-over" sounds like something deliberate. This is not like a ballet step; it is reflexive. It just happens.

Friends who saw Aaron usually marveled at how much better he seemed. "He's cured! No more Parkinson's," they would say. But while he did appear to be free of the disease, he was fainting again, falling and hurting himself. He'd been off dopamine for over a year. We went to see his doctor, Peter Warriner, in Boston.

"Do you think he had West Nile or Lyme disease?" I asked.

After a thorough examination, Dr. Warriner said, "No way." Looking at Aaron, he said, "You still have core Parkinson's, which

Soaking up the moments with Jordan.

accounts for your plunging blood pressure. But you're in outstanding shape." Still, since he had a mild case of the disease, the doctor put him back on a low dose of dopamine.

Three months later, in February, Aaron came with me to Russia. I went to do a story on Pussy Riot, the all-woman punk rock group. Our last night in Moscow, Aaron was sick, with sharp pains in his stomach. By the time we got to the airport the next morning, the throbbing was so insistent, he could barely walk. He broke into a sweat. "I think we should go to the hospital," he moaned.

I had done a story on Soviet medicine. I begged him, "Not a Russian hospital. If you can possibly get on the plane, we should."

Once in the air, Aaron popped an Ambien and slept—restlessly—most of the way. By the time we landed, I was punishing myself: did I make the right call about flying home? We went directly to the emergency room at New York–Presbyterian Hospital.

"I know it's what Clyde had," said Aaron, referring to his father, as he climbed up onto a gurney. "It's a twisted colon, or cancer."

"You don't know that," I said.

An alarmingly young-looking Dr. Morena palpated his stomach and said with some urgency, "You need an X-ray—now." A surgeon was summoned. "He has a blockage. Could be serious." It *was* a twisted colon. Within minutes he was wheeled to an OR. My life was now in someone else's hands.

The emergency room surgeon came to see me after the operation. He'd removed a long stretch of Aaron's colon. "It was about to burst," he said. "If you'd waited a few more hours, he'd have died."

The next day, Aaron's Parkinson's tremors were back. Other symptoms returned as well. By March his left hand was shaking dramatically, his facial tic was active, and he had a new diagnosis: "Parkinsonism."

After a few weeks of recuperation, Aaron felt well enough to travel to LA for Jordan's second birthday. During one of our dinners Taylor tried to get Jordan to tell us some good news. But being two, she took the command to perform as another opportunity to say no. Finally Taylor, pretending to be Jordan, said in falsetto: "I'm going to have a baby sister."

I paused, confused. "What? You're not . . . you—are you . . . pregnant?" I stuttered, not fully comprehending. Taylor was an only child. I guess I assumed Jordan would be too.

"You're not excited," said Tay. It came out, *J'accuse*.

"I am. I am."

"We just found out!" said Andrew, beaming.

"She's only four weeks old," said Tay.

"She? A sister? No, no. I think it's a brother," I said confidently. "I feel it." Then we all agreed that Jordan was going to be impossible.

Eight months later, on September 11, 2013, two days past Tay's due date, Aaron and I were on a plane to LA. We knew by then that I'd been wrong: it was a girl—so much for grandmotherly clairvoyance—and her name would be Chloe, after Aaron's dad, Clyde. I usually relax on planes, which is a good thing since I'm on them so often for my job. With no e-mail and no phones, I make a little aerie around my seat with stacks of reading (I still like to read on paper so I can underline). But concentrating on that flight was out of the question. I was too antsy: Would Taylor have a tough time again? Would Chloe be as perfect as Jordan? And I worried about her reaction to the baby. As an older sister myself, I knew how hard it was going to be for her to share. My mother loved to tell stories of how I tried to climb into my brother's crib and strangle him.

Taylor was doing everything she could *not* to go into labor that day: "I wouldn't want her to have 9/11 as her birthday." So it was with much relief that she went to bed that night with no hint of a contraction. But just in case, Aaron and I slept in their guest room over the garage instead of a hotel. Good thing, because my cell phone went off at 1:10 a.m. I could hear the pain in Taylor's voice: "We're going to the hospital." It was, luckily, Thursday, September 12—neither 9/11 nor Friday the thirteenth.

With Aaron still asleep, I crept downstairs and got into Taylor and Andrew's bed so if Jordan woke up, I'd be nearby.

Less than two hours later my cell rang again. "She's here! Chloe came!" Tay's voice was strong. There was no hint of the exhaustion she'd had after delivering Jordan.

"You just left," I said excitedly.

"I know! She just popped right out."

"Is she beautiful?"

"She looks like a little old man."

After Jordan went to preschool, Aaron and I left for Cedars-Sinai. "Let me look, let me see her," I said, charging into the hospital room. Tay was in bed cradling the baby, whose small round head was framed by the same pink and blue knit cap the nurses had put on Jordan. I had been whizzing with energy, but at the sight of Chloe, so delicate and innocent, everything in me slowed. Once again, I was rushed by supercharged emotions and a sense of wonder that so suddenly there was a whole new person.

Before I could hold Chloe, I had to sanitize my hands—on Taylor's orders. I really do wonder how on earth my daughter survived all the germs I carried, the wine I drank when I was pregnant and the general carelessness I subjected her to. At last, I held the sweet new angel in my arms, got to rock her and talk to her. I could feel myself succumbing to the seductiveness of her vulnerability.

Initially, I didn't think Chloe was as mesmerizingly beautiful as Jordan had been. But then Aaron scrolled through his iPhone and pulled up pictures of Jordan on her first day. "Look at that!" I said to Aaron. Dang. She hadn't been much of a looker either. My mother once told me that she thought I—*her* firstborn—was the prettiest baby ever, even as everyone else gazed at me with horror: I had a wry neck and looked almost deformed. "I never saw it," Dolly said. All of which reminds me of that old journalism adage, slightly paraphrased: "If your mom says you were beautiful, check it out." Same goes for grandmothers.

So much was different this time. With Jordan, Taylor was in such discomfort she could hardly get herself out of the bed. Now she was walking around jauntily and even took a shower. And there was none of that adrenalized sense of being on high alert.

Then there was Jordan's reaction to her new baby sister. Late that afternoon, as she approached the hospital room, we heard her, out in the hallway, say to Gigi, her nanny, "Mommy popped out Chloe like a balloon!"

Holding Chloe for the first time, September 12, 2013.

She ran into the room, revved up, hollering, "Where's Chloe? I want to see Chloe!" Then, tiptoeing to the bassinet, she peered in. "Why is she sleeping?" she asked, and made funny faces, trying to wake her up.

"I want to hold her," she said, climbing up on the bed. Taylor picked up Chloe from the bassinet and transferred her gingerly to Jordan's lap.

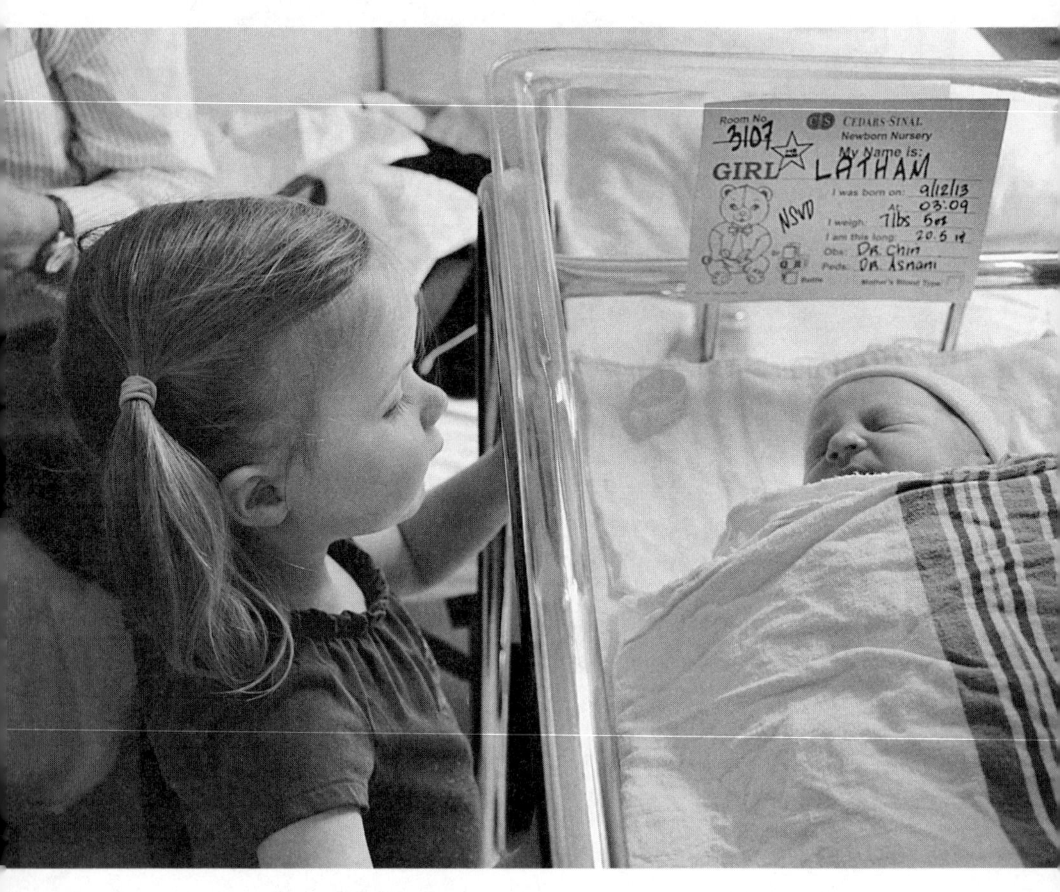

Jordan meeting her brand-new sister, September 12, 2013.

"Let go, Mummy."

"I can't. She's too little. I have to hold her head."

And with that, Jordan had had enough. She paid no mind to her baby sister for the rest of the day.

Jennie Held, my *60 Minutes* teammate, told her two-year-old, Juliet, that having a baby brother would be fun. "Big mistake," Jennie told me, "because newborns *aren't* fun. What they are are blobs that just sleep and poop and cry. And have Mommy's attention." That pretty much sums it up.

Aaron and I had bought Jordan a present for the occasion, something we knew she would love: a purple makeup kit with a plastic change purse, kiddie lipstick, a compact, a play iPhone, car keys, a credit card and a pair of glamorous pink movie-star sunglasses. "Princess stuff!" she said ecstatically, and played with it for the rest of the afternoon.

The next day we helped bring Chloe home, and almost immediately everyone diverted their attention from her to Jordan. Jennie Held told me that she was so worried about Juliet's jealousy, she came close to neglecting her newborn. We were doing the same.

Tay had gift-wrapped two packages for Jordie. "They're from Chloe," she said. The first was a helmet, the second, a pink scooter. "Daddy, Daddy. Let's go try it!" Jordan cried while Chloe snoozed away in her cradle, the forgotten one.

When she woke up, Jordan was gentle and sweet with her but once again quickly lost interest. I was relieved that she was more bored by Chloe than jealous. In fact, she looked off into space.

Jordan hugging her little sister.

"What're you thinking about?" Andrew asked her.

"Purple."

That night Jordan insisted we treat her like a little baby, as she tried to climb into Chloe's bassinet.

Taylor and Andrew had both been too busy to read up on how to explain a new baby is coming. Tay was working as vice president of development at Double Feature Films and Andrew had only recently changed careers from writing for a TV series to the wine business. He was building a client roster as a wine agent in Los Angeles and making his own Pinot Noir in Paso Robles. My point is that given the demands of their jobs and Jordan, they hadn't given much thought to incorporating number two.

If they had read up on it, they would have seen that much of the advice is intuitive: if you make any room changes, do it weeks before the sibling's due date, and don't be surprised if your toddler reverts to baby talk.

Aaron and I stayed in LA for a week this time. Taylor and Andrew needed less help, since Gigi was there for Jordan, and Taylor felt better and was more confident.

On Sunday, while we were there, their good friends Marc and Marti Resteghini brought over brunch. Marti had recently had a baby herself. She looked right at me and announced, "I ate my placenta."

Excuse me?

She said it's the new thing. You eat it or swirl it into a smoothie. I could hardly breathe. She claimed it wards off postpartum depression and hastens healing.

Taylor said the nurse in the birthing room asked if she wanted to eat *her* placenta. "No way," said Tay. "But," the nurse said, "it's the best placebo ever!"

Over the next two years, I would find myself feeling sorry for Chloe. Every little thing Jordan did as an infant had been oohed at and wowed over. She was planted in the spotlight, held constantly, stared at, marveled at. And here was Chloe, often left alone in her rocker, with a mobile to swat at, while we all reassured Jordan we still adored her.

On Thanksgiving weekend, Jordan bit Chloe. Again I understood that old aphorism about grandparents and grandchildren having a common enemy. It isn't that Jordan shouldn't have been reprimanded, but with every finger wag and scolding accusation I felt as if Taylor were thrusting hot pokers into me. Jordan was heaving with sobs as Taylor lit into her. Finally, she was allowed to crawl into Mommy's lap. "You have to promise you'll never do that again," said a very stern Taylor. "You're Chloe's big sister. You have to protect her, not hurt her, okay?" A pathetic little nod. "Now go kiss her and tell her you're sorry." Sibling rivalry changes parents. Chastising her little girl must have affected how Taylor saw herself. My sunny-tempered daughter became an occasional scold and I, not having raised two kids, was of little help. I was always flummoxed when I used to be asked, "How do you discipline Taylor?" We didn't. We never had to. I knew it sounded preposterous, but it was the truth. Of course, she was an only child. In my own childhood the only time I heard "Go to your room" or "Wait till your father gets home" was when my brother and I had a fight, or together made a mess.

Whenever Tay and company come to New York, our apartment is a shambles within one day. Just the way I hate it. Water bottles on my nice end tables, Starbucks coffee cups on the piano, Chloe's rocker scratching the coffee table, the floors slopped with Jordie's books, dolls and games. No one moves to straighten up. Not even me.

I continue to be Jordan's reader, which I love. Her favorite books at two and a half were *Rosie Revere, Engineer* by Andrea Beaty and *Dear Tooth Fairy* by Alan Durant.

Reading her one of the Berenstain Bears books, I pointed to a picture of Papa Bear on a river. "He's in a canoe," I said.

"No, it's a boat."

"Well, it's a kind of boat. A canoe."

"No, Lolly. I call it a boat."

Jordan's pastime was setting off cannonades of no's and don'ts. "Don't say dat, Daddy," she upbraided Andrew. Or "Don't touch my chair, Lolly." There isn't a grandma alive who hasn't gritted her teeth through that phase.

But then there were her fantasies, her intricate, magical rescue stories that she'd act out to charm the heavens.

"Play with me, Lolly," she would say, introducing me to her princess friends in her make-believe kingdoms: Ariel, Snow White, Cinderella and a unicorn, crowded together in a pink plastic castle.

"You're the teacher," she said as if she were Mike Nichols directing me on Broadway.

"Is this a school? A school for princesses?" I asked.

"Yes, and I'm the princess costume teacher," she explained.

Then she made us tea. When I complained that it was too hot, she shook her head. "Lolly, it's pretend tea!"

I was devoting myself to Jordan so much that at one point Taylor glowered at me and said, "Mom, you're going to have to stop calling Chloe 'the other one.'"

A college friend of mine who has eight grandchildren had already warned me that a grandmother's challenge is to make each of her grandchildren feel she loves them best. She said she learned from her father the importance of treating all the children equally. In his will he left his granddaughters more money than his grandsons, stating, "I liked them better."

"Honestly?" I asked.

"Yup. That's what he did. It wasn't good."

Taylor and Andrew decided it was time Jordan gave up her pacifier, which she called Ma. If I'd been brave I would have interceded: "Hey, Taylor, we never took yours away from you. You had it till you were four." But not a word.

After preparing Jordan for a week, they told her the Ma Fairy was coming for her pacifier that night. When my angel woke up the next morning her ma was gone. The fairy had left behind a pink tea set and a thank-you note.

Hard to believe, but it worked.

Once Chloe could travel, the family came to New York, as they did after Jordan was born. Taylor was breast-feeding every few hours again and pumping. She was so worn out that whenever I could, I'd spell her so she could get some sleep. I love that a grandmother's role is still taking care of our own kids. We grammas are still mommies.

And grampas are still daddies. Aaron gave Taylor time to rest as well. He took to holding Chloe, staring into her bright blue gaze as she grabbed for his glasses and put her fingers in his mouth. He says she was the most responsive infant he had ever seen. As with Jordan, his tremor calmed her.

Over the last year, Aaron's Parkinson's had gained ground. Andrew heard about a special boxing program for people with Parkinson's. Aaron tried it and liked it, so he began taking the subway to Brooklyn three nights a week, to Gleason's, the legendary old gym where Muhammad Ali trained and Robert De Niro got himself in shape for *Raging Bull*. It has enough grunge and professional boxers in training to elevate the game for Aaron and his twelve or so fellow Parkinsonians at various stages of the disease. The instructors persuade these men and women that they *can* do what they thought they couldn't—punch, squat, jump, and dance like Ali.

Aaron says that PD is a shrinking disease. "Your handwriting constricts in size and clarity, your body seems to get smaller as you slouch and stoop, your voice gets softer and softer until people can't hear you. All of which seems to marginalize you." Boxing is the opposite, he says. "The gloves give you the hands of a giant. And all the exercises we do are designed to pump you up." Since he's been in the class he's less stiff, with better balance and reduced tremors. "Also," he said, "we PDers get in a mental fetal position. Our new larger sense of ourselves helps us uncurl our brains, our attitudes, and our confidence."

Watching Aaron fight his way through this challenge, battling his own body, I think of something one of the interviewees in Michael Apted's *Up* series says: life is an act of courage.

After about six months in the ring, Aaron went for his regular checkup with his neurologist, who was amazed by the improvement. Even Aaron's Parkinsonian mask had lifted. To have the doctor confirm the changes clinically was reassuring. It meant it wasn't just wishful thinking.

So Aaron is on his second Parkinson's vacation. He still has a tremor in his left hand and he still has to take dopamine. But he walks faster, writes more legibly, stands up straighter and doesn't fall anymore. It's a TKO.

Like most grandparents, we had searched Chloe's face to see if she had inherited any of our features. Did she look like Dolly? My dad? Anyone in Aaron's family? So far as we could tell, the answer was no. But when she was three months old she began sprouting little wisps of red hair. "I was a redhead!" said Aaron, twinkling. Taylor looks exactly like Aaron. Chloe too? This was definitely annoying.

Chloe's personality was also sprouting. One day Andrew was tossing her in the air and out came a sustained, adult-sounding belly laugh. He threw her down on the bed, and she roared again. Taylor captured the laugh on her iPhone and sent it to us in New York. I don't think I'd ever seen a baby that young laugh so heartily. She was cracking up as if her daddy had told her the funniest joke she'd ever heard. Jordan never did that. There is no question that babies arrive, as a friend put it, with their bags already packed. Bags of personalities and dispositions.

I had worried I might not be able to love a second grandchild as much as the first, but in no time Chloe was just as unputdownable as Jordan. I loved smelling her downy head and feeling her little body against mine. The ultimate bonding came when she was a year old. She was in my arms as I walked her around my living room, pointing things out. "Flower." "Picture of Mommy." She was getting heavy, but when Taylor offered to relieve me, Chloe clung to me and wouldn't let go, not even for her mother's arms. This is exactly what you live for. I swelled with that warm flutter, the grandmother infatuation. I was falling in love again, but this is a love that never fades, never goes gray.

Don't tell me this is just hormone hydrology. Holding Chloe, I tried to remember who, except for Jordan, I had hugged like that in years. I air-kiss my friends and embrace Taylor, but only for seconds. With Jordan and Chloe it's sustained. I bring them inside the ropes of my private space, up against my heart, and hold on. It's a fleshy loving that's not sexual, and it feels so damn good. It must be why I crave these creatures so much.

Now I had two little girls I loved in a way I had never loved before.

Taylor and Andrew, a talented photographer, are always taking pictures of the girls and posting them on Facebook and Instagram, like the rest of their generation. At first they used Andrew's Nikon D7000, but they soon switched to their iPhones. "Look at Daddy," Tay says. "Chloe-bo, smile." "Jordie, hug your sister."

It reminds me of a joke Marvin Kalb once told me: Mrs. Himmelfarb, walking down the street, bumps into her old friend Mrs.

Ford, who's pushing her grandson in a stroller. "Oh, my, isn't he adorable!" says Mrs. Himmelfarb.

"If you think he's adorable here," says Mrs. Ford, "you should see his pictures!"

How much of children's lives today are experienced posing? In the middle of a romp in the playground, how often are kids asked to stop the action and look into Daddy's machine?

I met a gran who was on a tear about this, telling me that the kids are going to grow up and resent it. Not only the constant click-clicking, but all the embarrassing photos posted indelibly on the Internet.

"It's an invasion of their privacy," she said heatedly. "We took a million pictures of our kids, but they went into albums. They weren't put on YouTube. It's a generational thing. This constant picture-taking—they're all exploiting their kids."

"What about all the gadgets?" I asked. "The iPads, the apps, the mobile this and wearable that. They're addictive and isolating. Surely this technology is rewiring the kids' brains, maybe hampering their intellectual development."

She shook her head. How had we cool dudes of the 1970s become grumpy old women, put off by the newfangled? I remember how television (especially television news) used to be denigrated. It was going to dumb us all down. (Did it?)

"We're becoming fussbudgets," I said.

"Maybe we are," she said. "But I don't care." She then took on FaceTime. "Who wants to be having their dinner with some horrible lens in their face, being asked to perform for their grandparents?"

"How much of this have you said to your son and daughter-in-law?" I asked.

"Oh, gosh. Are you kidding? None of it. I'm like everyone else. I zip it."

Chloe was crawling, pulling herself up onto her feet, exploring and reaching for the very items you don't want a baby getting her hands on, including whatever Jordan was playing with.

One afternoon in LA, Jordan was painting a poster on the kitchen floor and telling me she was afraid her baby sister was going to smudge it by crawling all over it. So I picked up Chloe and walked her around until my arms ached (so much for my weight lifting twice a week) and I had to put her down, at which point she scampered over to Jordan and made a mess of the poster. It's not easy having a younger sibling. I could only empathize with Jordan.

How formative is "You love her more"? I suspect it's at the heart of us, one of the unappreciated forces in character development. We have profound effects on our brothers and sisters and they on us. After all, we spend more time with one another growing up than with our parents, especially if they both work. We shape each other as we compete for love, attention and approval. As Erica E. Goode put it, "Sibling relationships—and eighty percent of Americans have at least one—outlast marriages, survive the death of parents, resurface after quarrels that would sink any friendship."

In Jordan's case, we were wrong to assume she would have a

At the park with Jordan and Chloe.

miserable time adjusting to the interloper. She is gentle and loving with her sister—except when Chloe grabs for what she's playing with. When the girls fight, it's usually over possessions. Siblings compete for toys. There may be fifty for them to choose from, but they only want the one their sister or brother is playing with.

Little kids, starting early, are covetous. If a sibling grabs for their toy, they will be moved by a sense of unfairness. "Hey, that's *mine*." Or "I was playing with it," said in a tone of moral outrage. I did a story for *60 Minutes* with Shari Finkelstein in 2012 about how infants are born with built-in radar for injustice, for right and wrong. Studies have shown that children as young as one year old are acutely sensitive to how they're being treated in relation to their siblings. Their little antennas are up, searching for who's Mommy's favorite. So psychologists tell parents—and, by extension, grandparents—never let on if you do prefer one, and try to ignore the children's squabbles. Do not take sides; do not get involved at all. Let the kids argue and learn how to work out their differences on their own. If you must step in, out of fear of bodily harm, do not place blame. If a child detects one-sidedness, he or she may become a prizewinning acter-outer.

I'm remembering my last big fight with my brother, Jeff, who was sixteen months younger than I. He was nine, I was ten. Being considerably larger and stronger, I got on top of him and began to pummel. He looked up at me and said, "But I love you." (I'm in tears writing this.)

As usual Aaron and I spent the month of July 2015 with Taylor, Andrew and the girls. Andrew fulfilled his role as brigadier general of horseplay, carrying Chloe around upside down and spinning her in the air. Between her howls of laughter she kept saying, "Again, again!"

"Me too, Daddy," said Jordan. "Me too." With one child, the lines are straight; with two, everything's a braid.

Chloe, almost two, was beginning to talk, mixing her rapidly expanding vocabulary with hand signals to make herself understood. I was surprised at how often she played with Jordan. Once she could walk and run, the sisters jumped on a small trampoline together, laughing themselves silly. Or chased each other around the dining room table, screaming with fun.

Chloe was still mostly in the parallel-play phase but would go along when Jordan enlisted her into her fantasies: "I'm the doctor and you're sick." Occasionally Chloe, the more aggressive one, would punch Jordan. It's really hard not to interfere and adjudicate.

Jordan, at four and a half, often took my hand, steered me to her room and said, "Lolly, come play with me." She had built a cave out of couch pillows and insisted I crawl inside. Not easily done. Then there was the time she summoned all of us to her puppet show about a mermaid and an elephant. When Chloe wandered into the middle of the performance, Jordan howled in protest. Neither Tay nor Andrew did much more than roll their eyes. The only time either of them raised their voice was when one of the girls hit the other. I, on the other hand, was suffering from a throat ailment: choking—to keep me from constantly hollering, "*Stop that!*"

We were in LA for Grandparents' Day at Jordan and Chloe's school. Each child had only one grandparent or one pair of grandparents in attendance. How quaint. I scoured the crowd, checking out who looked older than we did. I'm sure everyone there was doing the same.

Before our lunch of peanut butter sandwiches and grapes, Jordan and the other four-year-olds put on a show. As they started singing "You Are My Sunshine," a much younger little redhead wandered onto the stage. It was Chloe! But instead of shooing her away, Jordan waved her over and put her arm around her shoulders. Oh no. Was it an embrace? Or a headlock? But then, with "You make me happy when skies are gray," Jordan bent down and kissed Chloe, who reached up and kissed her back.

"Do you like having a sister?" I asked Jordan later.

"It's wonderful," she said.

"Why do you say that?" I was a little surprised, given all the bickering.

"I play with her, and she likes me."

I wanted to smother her with hugs.

"She cries a lot," Jordan added, "but I still like to play with her so much. I love her."

Jordan and Chloe, the best of friends at Chloe's second birthday party, 2015.

Chloe, Taylor, Jordan and Andrew.

TEN

A Call to Arms

If we want things to stay as they are,
things will have to change.
—GIUSEPPE DI LAMPEDUSA, *The Leopard*

In April 2015 I attended a Republican focus group in New Hampshire run by the pollster Frank Luntz. I was interested in whether Hillary Clinton's being a grandmother would soften perceptions of her.

At my request, Frank asked the group: "What one word comes to mind when I say 'grandmother'?" Here's what they said: "warm," "hugs," "wonderful," "happiness," "cookies," "sweet," "love," "food," "fun," "spoiling," "cozy," "nurturing," "unconditional acceptance."

It was unclear whether any of those images were going to rub off on the Democratic candidate. Probably not among those Republicans. But one thing was clear: It wasn't going to hurt Hillary to show up with little Charlotte in her arms at every single whistle stop from now till the election. (We hear so much about the Hispanic vote or the evangelical vote, but almost nothing about grandmothers as a bloc.)

As a group, we grandmothers have a five-star reputation. And we are at a juncture where we have an obligation to put it to use in our grandchildren's lives. On my journey of researching and interviewing I came to appreciate how essential, how vital we are in promoting their health and happiness. In fact, as grandparents we owe our very existence to our roles of providing our adult children with backup and our grandchildren with comfort.

So I am issuing a call to arms to all grandparents: If you're not already pitching in, start now; become actively engaged in your grandchildren's lives. If you're already babysitting and sending money, do more. If you live in another state, build into your retirement plan a way to be with those children more often. And if the path to your own grandchildren is blocked for whatever reason, then get involved helping other young children.

I'm also calling on parents of young children who are denying or curtailing grandparent access: ease up (except in cases of egregious physical or mental abuse). It's time to be forgiving. Swallow hard, if that's what it takes, "for the sake of the children."

Quite simply, they need us. And just as important, our children, coping with the compounded stress of parenting and working, need us. Fortuitously, we're in a situation where supply and demand mesh: they need our help just as many of us find we have the time. We have added thirty years to our lifespans in the last century, and many seniors have not figured out what to do with those surplus seasons.

I was discussing this with Dr. Linda Fried, dean of the Mailman School of Public Health at Columbia University, who has spent years thinking about this new, undefined stage in human history.

"I only know a few people who don't want them, the extra years," she says with a laugh. "Nobody's gonna turn them down!"

She explained that our lives are now split thirty-thirty-thirty. We spend the first thirty years on education, the middle thirty on work and the last thirty—well, they're a big question mark. "The challenge of our time," she said, "is to design and build that last stage of life that we never had before.

"The elderly are the only increasing natural resource in the entire world," said Fried. I love that. We're a surplus value! Using that value to help grandchildren is a perfect solution, and the advantages for our overly stretched daughters, daughters-in-law, sons and sons-in-law are immeasurable. "They're in that middle thirty, in the thirty-thirty-thirty equation," she said, "when they're working *and* raising children. It's crazy-making. They're always tired and anxious."

Many of us have the wherewithal and the energy to step up our involvement. Thanks to modern medicine, we're not just living longer, we're living healthy longer. So while we may need hip replacements and cataract operations, get age spots and thinning hair, lose our waists, and sag, well, everywhere . . . there are remedies. The new hips make you limber again; you see 20/20; you can have the spots lightened and wear a wig. At seventy many of us can still chase around after a four-year-old.

And we grandparents have so much to give. Beyond affection and financial support, we have become what the Bible calls *zikna*, meaning one who has acquired wisdom. Why not channel what we have learned to our grandchildren? When we're in their lives, it can be win-win-win. While we're contributing to the grandkids' general welfare, they do the same for us. They keep us young.

Data in a new study even suggest that postmenopausal women who take care of their grandchildren have less dementia.

When I told psychiatrist Anna Fels I was urging grandmas to spend the last third of their lives helping with the grandchildren, she brought me up short.

"Would you have wanted *your* mother doing that? We have this ideal of grandparents helping. It doesn't always work," she said.

But I'm not saying your mother or mother-in-law should *move in*. Just that there be some reasonable amount of contact. I understand the need to find some balance. Honestly, I would not have wanted Dolly integrated into my life when I was younger. But, as they say, life's a trade-off. Maybe Gramma moves near, but not *too* near. Sees the grandchildren often, but not *too* often, or while you're not there.

If Gran does want to move nearby, there are bound to be some howls from a wife to her husband: "Your mother here? Oh my god." Or from a sister: "You're letting your mother-in-law live next door?" Or the inevitable from a friend: "You know, you'll end up taking care of her when she gets really old."

Maybe. But in some ways it would be worse if she lived across the country. You're still going to end up taking care of her. When my mother got "really old," I flew to see her in Swampscott every other weekend, and that was long before her final illness. As her friends began dying, one by one, she began to wither from the lack of companionship. Like Rich Bonin's mom, she was watching a lot of television, just waiting for the sun to go down. The weight on me from not doing more, seeing her more often, was draining.

During this journey, I kept running into rejected grans, either banished altogether from their grandchildren's lives or confined to few and short visits. Several young couples told me, "I'm protecting my kids from *that* woman"—meaning their mother—or "*those* people" (gramps included). But so often they were spiting themselves and depriving the kids of all that love.

To our sons and daughters who keep the grandparents at arm's length: you should realize that we (most of us, anyway) don't grandparent the way we raised you. How often do daughters say they don't recognize their own mothers (see Michelle Obama) as they pivot from the disciplinarian to the great indulger? Hell, we don't even recognize ourselves! So if we were rough on you, hypercritical, interfering, smothering—we probably aren't any of those things with the babies. One look at that child and we find our critical thoughts have been incapacitated.

So give us a second chance. Shake off your hostility, and keep remembering that your kids will benefit. And in the end so will you.

And here's another thought: when you let a gran help out, your relationship with her is likely to improve. Betsey Stevenson said in our conversation, "At the end of a full day of working, you come home, and if your mother-in-law's been babysitting, you might find yourself overcome by gratitude. And when you see how much your child loves his or her grandmother, how can it not affect the relationship in a positive way?"

Grans, you also need to sit on your grievances. Look, we all know we made mistakes as parents. Okay—so admit it. Don't let the verdict of restricted access stand. Take it to the appeals court, and be humble. Grovel. You may have to act like a defeated army that surrenders unconditionally. Think Germany after World War II. They got the Marshall Plan; you'll get those babies!

And here's something else: mood and overall sense of well-being tend to improve with age; most of us get nicer with maturity, more agreeable. According to Paul Costa of the long-running Baltimore Longitudinal Study of Aging, "No more than ten percent of the elderly fall into the stereotype of being depressed, cranky, irritable and obsessed with their alimentary canal."

In fact, it appears that we humans are at our *un*happiest in our late thirties and forties. We bottom out in our early fifties, then keep getting happier through our sixties and seventies and even beyond, until disability kicks in. What this tells me is that babies are being raised by people in the unhappiest phase of their lives. Which makes it all the more important that we happy, satisfied *zikna* step in.

Of all the interviews I conducted, all the articles I read, all the personal experiences I had with my own granddaughters, one conversation stands out. It was with psychologist Nancy Davis in Bradenton, Florida. She told me that she always asks her patients the question "Who loved you?"

"If nobody loved you in your first five or six years," she told me, "you're screwed. There's a hole in you that never gets filled. It's like you can't know what love is unless somebody loves you during that time."

"Is it enough if the answer is 'My grandmother loved me'?" I asked.

"It's enough."

That's because a grandmother's love is wholesome and consummate. What I experienced with the births of Jordan and Chloe—that staggering thunderbolt of joy—is pretty universal. One day we may be clever enough to do autopsies of emotions. There'll be love coroners! And we'll be able to dissect this grandparent tingling, give it a solid definition. Right now it's so mysteriously pure it's as impossible to define as a quark.

And yet it is open and easy for our grandchildren to read. They sense its unconditionality and gravitate to it. And the great reward, the extra bonus points in these last thirty years, is they love us back.

"Oh my God. It's amazing how much kids love their grandmothers," said Betsey Stevenson. "It's just this wonderful, wonderful, special thing."

Grandchildren are the dessert course of life, or, as Steve Leber, who founded Grandparents.com, told me, "God gave us grandchildren to make up for aging."

Ain't it the truth.

Acknowledgments

My deep thanks and appreciation to:

The dozens of grandmothers who confided in me, many of whom are my girlfriends and colleagues. I love you for your honesty and generosity.

The scientists and doctors who contributed: biochemists, anthropologists, psychologists and public health officials. Special appreciation to Louann Brizendine, whose books and conversations were central to my education, as well as Wednesday Martin, Dr. Katie Hinde, Dr. James Bates and Dr. Linda Fried.

My friends and colleagues who read the pages, for their invaluable advice—Joni Evans, Rich Bonin, Jeff Fager, Shachar Bar-On, Peggy Noonan—and Phyllis Grann for her expert eye.

My editor at Blue Rider Press, Sarah Hochman, and publisher David Rosenthal, who gave me the idea in the first place.

My agent and friend Esther Newberg, for her encouragement and steadfastness.

Researchers Perry Wilson and Maria Rutan, for holding things together, including me.

The utmost thanks go to my husband, Aaron Latham, for reading every chapter, over and over.

And most especially to my daughter and son-on-law, Taylor and Andrew, for allowing me to invade their lives.

Notes

OVER THE RIVER AND THROUGH THE WOODS

Page 2. Baby boomer women alone . . . Judith A. Seltzer and Jenjira J. Yahirun, "Diversity in Old Age: The Elderly in Changing Economic and Family Context," in *Diversity and Disparities: America Enters a New Century*, ed. John R. Logan (New York: Russell Sage Foundation, 2014), 290.

Page 3. . . . the road to breaking the glass ceiling. Liza Mundy, "Playing the Granny Card," *The Atlantic*, October 2015.

Page 3. Hanna Rosin wrote . . . Hanna Rosin, "Old People Are Cool," *The Atlantic*, July 2015.

Page 3. Research shows that people . . . Mundy, "Playing the Granny Card."

CHAPTER ONE. LIFE AND DEATH

Page 9. Roughly translated, it means . . . FDR is said to have had "a hyperthymic personality." Thomas Mallon, "Are All of Our Leaders Mad?" *New York Times Book Review*, August 21, 2011.

Page 20. The hormones cause a new mother . . . Alan Anderson and Lucy Middleton, "Love Special: What Is This Thing Called Love?" *New Scientist*, April 26, 2006.

Page 23. As *The New York Times* reported . . . David Sanger and Michael Gordon, "Clearing Hurdles to Iran Nuclear Deal with Standoffs, Shouts and Compromise," *New York Times*, July 16, 2015.

Page 23. In various surveys . . . "Surprising Facts About Grandparents," Grandparents .com, based on MetLife survey, 2012.

Page 23. Most say being with their grandkids . . . Pew Research Center, "Getting Old in America: Expectation vs. Reality," June 29, 2009, 33.

Page 28. Dr. Brizendine told me . . . Anderson and Middleton, "Love Special."

CHAPTER TWO. GRANNY NANNIES

Page 29. During the 2008 campaign . . . Rachel L. Swarns, "Obama's Mother-in-Law to Move to White House," *New York Times*, January 1, 2009.

Page 30. . . . "you just hear a little bit too much." Holly Yeager, "The Heart and Mind of Michelle Obama," *O: The Oprah Magazine*, November 2007, 19, footnote 2.

Page 30. . . . helped with homework . . . Rachel L. Swarns, "An In-law Is Finding Washington to Her Liking," *New York Times*, May 4, 2009.

Page 30. She responded, "I have candy . . ." Scott Helman, "Holding Down the Family Fort," *Boston Globe*, March 30, 2008.

Page 30. Mrs. Obama said that the strict . . . Theresa Walker, "Here's to You, First Granny," *Orange County Register*, August 21, 2013.

Page 30. Unlike the rest of the family . . . Jodi Kantor, *The Obamas* (Boston: Little, Brown, 2012), 226–27.

Page 31. "They don't have much sex appeal." Judith Shulevitz, "Why Do Grandmothers Exist?" *New Republic*, January 29, 2013.

Page 32. In one study in rural Gambia . . . Natalie Angier, "Weighing the Grandma Factor: In Some Societies, It's a Matter of Life and Death," *New York Times*, November 5, 2002.

Page 32. Even the other primates . . . Margaret Walker and James Herndon, "Menopause in Non-Human Primates?" *Biology of Reproduction* 79 (May 2008).

Page 32. . . . are whales, dolphins, and elephants . . . James R. Cary and Catherine Gruenfelder, "Population Biology of the Elderly," in *Between Zeus and the Salmon: The Biodemography of Longevity*, ed. Kenneth Wachter and Caleb Finch (Washington, DC: National Academies Press, 1997), 127–60.

Page 33. But while her mother was miserable . . . Bharati Mukherjee, "Gained in Translation," in *Eye of My Heart* (New York: HarperLuxe, 2009), 261–64.

Page 37. There are even baby showers today . . . Charlotte Latvala, "Should You Have a Grandbaby Shower?" Grandparents.com.

Page 37. ***Stupendous, miraculous, unsurpassed . . .*** Ogden Nash, "First Child . . . Second Child," in *Selected Poetry of Ogden Nash: 650 Rhymes, Verses, Lyrics and Poems* (New York: Black Dog & Leventhal, 1995), 73.

Page 40. I actually read about an analysis . . . Vasyl Palchykov, Kimmo Kaski, Janos Kertész, Albert-László Barabási and Robin I. M. Dunba, "Sex Differences in Intimate Relationships," *Scientific Reports* 2, no. 370 (2012).

Page 45. And my daughter was evicted from the hospital . . . For centuries, the Chinese practiced a similar postpartum sequestration known as "sitting the month." New mothers were confined at home "under the stern glare of grandmothers and aunts who banned bathing, fresh air and certain foods." Dan Levin, "A Pampered Month Off for Mom," *New York Times*, October 3, 2015.

Page 47. Some grans read books . . . Nora Krug, "Technology Helping More Baby-Boomer Grandparents Stay Plugged In to Grandkids," *Washington Post*, October 31, 2014.

Page 47. Grandmothers are also tweeting . . . A MetLife report in 2012 found almost one-third of grandparents e-mail with their grandchildren, and a quarter use Facebook. Grandparents.com says 25 percent are texting their grandkids. One reason baby boomers are proficient on the Web and with apps is because so many of them are still in the workforce. Today's jobs so often demand tech savvy. From the Center for Family and Demographic Research at Bowling Green University in Ohio.

Page 54. One glamma told the *New York Times* . . . Joanne Kaufman, "When Grandma Can't Be Bothered," *New York Times*, March 5, 2009.

CHAPTER THREE. NATURAL ENEMIES

Page 63. In Italy almost a third of divorces . . . Hannah Seligson, *A Little Bit Married*, quoted in Terri Apter, *What Do You Want from Me?* (New York: W. W. Norton, 2009), 221.

Page 63. . . . "invading" the marital home. Apter, *What Do You Want from Me?*, 9.

Page 63. ". . . while your mother-in-law still lives." Juvenal, *The Sixteen Satires*, third edition. Trans. Peter Green (London: Penguin Books, 1998).

Page 63. One of the most bloodthirsty . . . *The Grimm Reader: The Classic Tales of the Brothers Grimm*, ed. Maria Tatar (New York: W. W. Norton, 2010), 273.

Page 65. And while the mother and the wife . . . Elizabeth Bernstein, "A Mother, a Son and a Wife," *Wall Street Journal*, May 20, 2013.

Page 65. ". . . Instead, he allowed her to compete . . ." Doris Kearns Goodwin, *No Ordinary Time* (New York: Simon & Schuster, 1994), 80.

Page 66. "If you'd just run your comb . . ." Geoffrey Ward and Ken Burns, *The Roosevelts: An Intimate History* (New York: Alfred A. Knopf, 2014), 196.

Page 68. Also, the new generation . . . Adam Minter, "China's In-Law Wars Hammer On," *Bloomberg*, June 28, 2012.

Page 69. . . . mean old crones took charge of the grandchildren. Alessandra Stanley, "On Indian TV, 'I Do' Means to Honor and Obey the Mother-in-Law," *New York Times*, December 25, 2012.

Page 71. "Not speaking your mind . . ." *Eye of My Heart: 27 Writers Reveal the Hidden Pleasures and Perils of Being a Grandmother,* ed. Barbara Graham (New York: Harper Luxe, 2009), 302.

Page 72. Pushing back, she may defy . . . Apter, *What Do You Want from Me?*, 167.

Page 72. "It makes no difference . . . " Graham, *Eye of My Heart*, 308.

Page 72. But the new mother hears . . . Apter, *What Do You Want from Me?*, 168.

Page 75. "She could blackmail me." Anna Fels, the psychiatrist, told me that far more painful for a grandmother than being cut off by a daughter-in-law is being denied by her own daughter.

Page 78. An educator recently told Taylor . . . Brad Zacuto, head of Westside Neighborhood School, Los Angeles.

Page 79. Indeed, she said of Sara . . . Joseph P. Lash, *Love, Eleanor: Eleanor Roosevelt and Her Friends* (Garden City, NY: Doubleday, 1982), 56.

Page 79. According to Bonnie Angelo . . . Bonnie Angelo, *First Mothers: The Women Who Shaped the Presidents* (New York: Harper, 2000), 5.

Page 79. Curtis wrote that this was unfair to Sara . . . Curtis Roosevelt, *Too Close to the Sun: Growing Up in the Shadow of My Grandparents, Franklin and Eleanor* (New York: Public Affairs, 2009), 67.

Page 80. She lavished the grandkids . . . Angelo, *First Mothers*, 24.

Page 80. . . . Alice . . . became a doting gran. Marc Peyser and Timothy Dwyer, *Hissing Cousins: The Untold Story of Eleanor Roosevelt and Alice Roosevelt Longworth* (New York: Doubleday, 2015).

Page 83. The men's symptoms faded . . . James S. Bates and Alan C. Taylor, "Grandfather Involvement and Aging Men's Mental Health," *American Journal of Men's Health* 6, no. 3 (May 2012).

Page 84. They got to see their grandchildren . . . Paul Vitello, "Parents of 9/11 Victims Torn from Grandchildren," *New York Times*, January 19, 2007.

Page 85. Laurine's husband, Al . . . Jan Goodwin, "The Grandparents of Newtown: A Grief Like No Other," *AARP The Magazine,* December 2013–January 2014.

CHAPTER FOUR. HOUSE IN THE BRONX

Page 89. As much as 60 percent . . . Pew Research. *Family Support in Graying Societies,* 2015.

Page 95. *I saw an old, forgotten man* . . . David Maraniss, *Barack Obama: The Story* (New York: Simon & Schuster, 2012), 317.

Page 96. In his biography of Obama . . . Maraniss, *Barak Obama*, 547.

Page 98. In February 2010 . . . Author interview with Rimas Jasin.

Page 107. The number of caretaker grandparents . . . Gretchen Livingston and Kim Parker, "Since the Start of the Great Recession, More Children Raised by Grandparents," Pew Research Center, September 9, 2012, 2.

Page 107. During the recession the largest increase . . . Paola Scommegna, "More U.S. Children Raised by Grandparents," Population Reference Bureau, March 2012.

Page 107. There's a misconception . . . Actually, about half are white; 34 percent are black; 18 percent are Hispanic. Caucasians are the group that's continuing to grow, primarily because of the economy. Livingston and Parker, "Since the Start of the Great Recession . . ."

Page 110. Anger is a typical symptom . . . Study by Laura Pittman at Northern Illinois University, cited in Scommegna, "More U.S. Children Raised by Grandparents."

Page 110. . . . "a buffer against the ruinous effects of adversity." Emily Bazelon, "A Question of Resilience," *New York Times Magazine,* April 30, 2006.

Page 110. But even for those without the 5-HTT mutation . . . Study at Yale of children removed from their homes because of physical or sexual abuse or neglect by Joan Kaufman, a professor of psychiatry at Yale Medical School in biological psychiatry, referred to in Bazelon, "A Question of Resilience."

Page 111. Paula wondered if being a single mom . . . As the economy has recovered, births among married women have increased again, but not among unmarried women. Yet despite those recent declines, single motherhood is still quite common: 40 percent of births in the US are to unmarried women and they are still more likely to be young, black or Latina and without a college degree. Claire Cain

Miller, "Single Motherhood, in Decline Overall, Rises for Women 35 and Older," *New York Times*, May 9, 2015.

CHAPTER FIVE. WORKING GRANNIES

Page 113. Together they allowed grandparents . . . MetLife, "Report on American Grandparents, July 2011."

Page 114. The millennials, aged twenty to thirty-five . . . Richard Fry, "More Millennials Living with Family Despite Improved Job Market," Pew Research Center, July 2015, 7.

Page 114. The dating site Match.com even . . . Dionne Searcey, "U.S. Millennials Less Likely to Leave the Nest," *New York Times*, July 30, 2015.

Page 121. They wanted to carve out undivided time . . . Motoko Rich, "It's the Economy, Honey," *New York Times*, February 11, 2012.

Page 122. . . . in Alabama, $5,547. Danielle Paquette, "The States Where Parents Spend the Most on Child Care," *Washington Post,* May 20, 2015. Only 9 percent of working women make more than $75,000.

Page 122. In most states high-quality child care . . . Daniel Marans, "Child Care Is More Expensive Than College in Most States," *Huffington Politics*, October 6, 2015.

Page 122. At some point in their lives . . . MetLife, "Women of Wealth, Financial Planning," February 2012.

Page 122. We've seen a seismic gender shift . . . M. P. Dunleavy, "Mars, Venus and the Handling of Money," *New York Times*, February 23, 2014.

Page 126. They're still working age. According to 2010 census data, 53 percent.

Page 126. Up to 60 percent of sixty-five-year-olds . . . From the 2008 Grandparents.com study: 60 percent of grandparents have a full-time or part-time job; nearly 25 percent have started their own business. The workforce over fifty-five is growing faster than any other age group. Rainer Stack, 2008.

Page 126. Same for all the action-hero sexagenarians . . . Manohla Dargis and A. O. Scott, "This Summer's Action Heroes Are Several Shades of Gray," *New York Times*, May 3, 2015.

Page 127. Most sixty- and seventy-year-olds have more money . . . St. Louis Fed study: since the financial crisis, incomes have risen for the elderly, while they have dropped for the young and middle-aged. Those sixty-two to sixty-nine gained 12.3 percent since 2007; for those who are seventy-plus, the increase was 15.6 percent. Meanwhile, their family expenses dropped: mortgages are paid off, children leave.

Washington Post, November 4, 2013. According to a May 2015 survey by the Pew Research Center, close to 70 percent of Americans over 65 say they either live comfortably or have enough to "meet their basic needs with a little left over for extras." Only 31 percent of those eighteen to forty-nine say they live "comfortably."

Page 127. No wonder so many keep working . . . One-fourth of all grandparents earn more than $90,000 a year; one-fourth earn less than $25,000. MetLife, "Report on American Grandparents," 14.

Page 127. That could be because about a third . . . Interestingly, their sons are slightly less educated: 28 percent are college graduates. Ibid., 13.

Page 127. Unlike their dads . . . Brigid Schulte, "You're Probably Too Busy to Read This," *Washington Post*, March 16, 2014. NYU sociologist Dalton Conley suggests that today's professions in technology, engineering and academics are similar to the pursuits of the mind that the ancient Greek philosophers envisioned as leisure.

Page 128. It's getting so difficult to keep up . . . K. C. Summers, "Grandparenting 101 for Baby Boomers," *Washington Post*, May 10, 2015.

Page 132. We're out there buying baby food . . . Cheryl L. Lampkin, "Insights and Spending Habits of Modern Grandparents," AARP report, March 2012. Two surveys: 53 percent help with education; 37 percent with everyday living expenses; 23 percent with medical or dental expenses. Many said even with the weaker economy, they still spend on the grandkids by cutting back in other places. The grandchildren have a higher priority.

Page 132. I am convinced there's a gramma gene . . . Grandparents.com., 2008, from their commissioned survey conducted by Peter Francese. One-third of all US consumer spending is by grandparents: $52 billion on their grandchildren in 2008; $17 billion just on clothes and toys.

Page 132. As a group, grandparents spend roughly $2.5 billion . . . MetLife, "Report on American Grandparents."

Page 138. But a surprising number of people over ninety . . . One theory about women's longevity is that many in our generation were put on hormone replacement therapy the second we got our first hot flash. Because estrogen strengthens bones, older women are apparently not breaking their hips as much.

CHAPTER SIX. MACHO TO MUSH

Page 147. Eighty percent of suicides . . . Lenny Bernstein and Lena H. Sun, "Older White Men Face Higher Suicide Risk," *Washington Post*, August 13, 2014.

Page 147. An article in the *American Journal of Men's Health* . . . James S. Bates and Alan C. Taylor, "Grandfather Involvement and Aging Men's Mental Health," *American Journal of Men's Health* 6, no. 3 (May 2012).

Page 154. I've heard of parents paying up to $30,000 . . . Anne Tergesen, "The Long (Long) Wait to Be a Grandparent," *Wall Street Journal*, March 31, 2014.

Page 154. He should describe the family's roots . . . Susanne Frost Olsen, Alan C. Taylor and Kelly DiSpirito Taylor, "An Irreplaceable Influence," *BYU Magazine*, Summer 2001.

Page 155. There's something about older men . . . Kirk Bloir, "What About Grandfathers?" Ohio State University Extension Seniors Series, Ohio Department of Aging. http://ohioline.osu.edu/ss-fact/0195.html.

Page 155. In polls, teenage boys . . . Dr. Virginia Wilton and Dr. Judith A. Davey, "Grandfathers—Their Changing Family Roles and Contributions," Blue Skies Fund, New Zealand Institute for Research on Ageing, March 2006.

Page 156. According to Louann Brizendine . . . Louann Brizendine, *The Male Brain* (New York: Three Rivers Press, 2010), 88.

Page 157. When moms and grannies do horseplay . . . Sue Shellenbarger, "Dad's Roughhousing Lessons: Fathers Teach Risk-Taking, Boundary-Setting," *Wall Street Journal*, June 11, 2014.

Pages 157. A father or grandfather's unpredictability . . . Paul Raeburn, *Do Fathers Matter? What Science Is Telling Us About the Parent We've Overlooked* (New York: Scientific American/Farrar, Straus and Giroux, 2014), 149.

Page 157. It's said that girls who were the most popular . . . Raeburn, *Do Fathers Matter?*, 152.

Page 158. His grandson Curtis said . . . Curtis Roosevelt, *Too Close to the Sun: Growing Up in the Shadow of My Grandparents, Franklin and Eleanor* (New York: Public Affairs, 2009), 15–16.

Page 158. ". . . didn't trouble FDR." Ibid., 15.

Page 162. Only two nephews had survived . . . Harold Werner, *Fighting Back* (New York: Columbia University Press, 1994).

Pages 163–65. As Aaron wrote, hospitals began offering . . . One in ten fathers suffers from moderate to severe postpartum depression. Raeburn, *Do Fathers Matter?,* 118.

Page 165. Testosterone builds all that is "male" . . . Brizendine, *The Male Brain*, xix.

Page 167. He's amused by everything . . . Ibid., 128.

Page 167. At the same time, the new dad's . . . Ibid., 104.

Page 168 . . . polarized by class. Virginia Wilton and Judith A. Davey, "Grandfathers—Their Changing Family Roles and Contributions," New Zealand Institute for Research on Ageing, Victoria University of Wellington, March 2006.

Page 176. That was that. Claire Cain Miller, "Single Motherhood, in Decline Overall, Rises for Women 35 and Older," *New York Times*, May 9, 2015.

Page 178. As Billy Witz wrote . . . Billy Witz, "At 67, Coughlin Proves a Taskmaster Can Be Tender," *New York Times*, September 1, 2013.

Page 179. . . . greater ability to develop and maintain friendships. Bloir, "What About Grandfathers?"

CHAPTER SEVEN. STEP-GRANDMOTHERS

Page 181. ***Step-grandmothers are one of the fastest growing* . . .** Twoofus.org, "Step Grandparents," http://www.twoofus.org/educationalcontent/articles/step-grandparents/index.aspx.

Page 183. "I was not prepared for the incandescent . . ." Quoted in Charles Krauthammer, "Motherhood Missed," *Aura*, May 12, 2000.

Page 183. A study on foster mothers . . . Johanna Bick, Damion Grasso, Mary Dozier and Kristin Bernard, "Foster Mother–Infant Bonding: Associations Between Foster Mothers' Oxytocin Production, Electrophysiological Brain Activity, Feelings of Commitment, and Caregiving Quality," *Child Development* 84, no. 3 (May/June 2013), 835.

Page 187. If the mother gives her permission . . . Wednesday Martin, "Why It's Easier to Love a Stepfather Than a Stepmother," *Psychology Today*, June 21, 2011. Research shows that kids have a harder time accepting a stepmother than a stepdad; that applies to step-grans as well.

Page 189. Will the second wife dilute . . . Gabe and Lipman-Blumen, *Making Adult Stepfamilies Work*, 209.

Page 194. I told her about a poll of stepmothers . . . Jeannette Lofas, *Stepparenting: Everything You Need to Know to Make It Work* (New York: Citadel Press, 2004), 9.

Page 195. A part of me rejoiced . . . Courtney Jung, "Overselling Breast-Feeding," *New York Times*, October 16, 2015. Interesting factoid: well-to-do white women are far more likely to breast-feed today than poor women of color.

Page 195. Some adult children are wise enough . . . Gabe and Lipman-Blumen, *Making Adult Stepfamilies Work*, 201–22.

CHAPTER EIGHT. HOPE MEADOWS: A ROAD TRIP

Page 200. What she found was distressing . . . Foster homes can often make things worse. Some chilling facts: children have been killed in state care five times more often than in their own homes, and abused three times more, according to Wes Smith, *Hope Meadows* (New York: Berkley Books, 2001), 250. Eighty percent of the inmates in Illinois prisons had once been in foster care, according to Dirk Johnson, "For Distant Generations in Illinois, Unrelated But Oh So Close," *New York Times*, September 15, 2008.

Page 204. Many contend with serious medical problems . . . Smith, *Hope Meadows*, 9.

Page 205. . . . compared with only 30 percent in foster care. According to the staff at Hope Meadows and Beth Baker, *With a Little Help from Our Friends: Creating Community as We Grow Older* (Nashville: Vanderbilt University Press, 2014), 103.

Page 205. Two of Irene's fellow grandparents . . . Smith, *Hope Meadows*, 112.

Page 213. ". . . my kids haven't ever seen it either." Currently the ratio of African-American and Hispanic to white children is 29:9. And among the adults, 15:32.

Page 213. . . . call them Gramma or Grampa. Vicki Mabrey, "Hope Meadows," *60 Minutes II*, April 17, 2002.

Page 213. "These are my kids." There are several other intergenerational communities around the country built on the Hope Meadows model, including New Life Village in Tampa, Florida; Bridge Meadows in Portland, Oregon; and Treehouse Community in Easthampton, Massachusetts. Others are in development.

Page 214. "They might not react like they do here." Johnson, "For Distant Generations."

Page 220. . . . if people have too much free time. John Maynard Keynes, "Economic Possibilities of Our Grandchildren," a 1930 essay quoted in Elizabeth Kolbert, "No Time," *The New Yorker,* May 26, 2014.

CHAPTER NINE. CHLOE

Page 245. As Erica E. Goode put it . . . Erica Goode, "The Secret World of Siblings," *U.S. World and News Report*, January 10, 1994.

Page 247. Studies have shown that children as young as one . . . Jane Mersky Leder, "Adult Sibling Rivalry," *Psychology Today*, January 1, 1993.

Notes

CHAPTER TEN. A CALL TO ARMS

Page 254. Data in a new study even suggest . . . There's an intriguing hitch: the highest cognitive performance was seen in women who spent one day a week minding grandchildren. Those who did it five days a week had lower working-memory performance and lower processing speed. In other words, don't overdo. K. F. Burn, V. W. Henderson, D. Ames, L. Dennerstein and C. Szoeke, "Role of Grandparenting in Postmenopausal Women's Cognitive Health: Results from the Women's Healthy Aging Project," *Menopause* 21, no. 10 (October 2014), PubMed .gov (PMID: 24714623).

Page 256. . . . nicer with maturity, more agreeable. Anne Tergesen, "Why Everything We Know About Aging Is Probably Wrong," *Wall Street Journal*, December 1, 2014; Elizabeth Bernstein, "And We Actually Get Nicer with Age," *Wall Street Journal*, April 22, 2014.

Page 256. We bottom out in our early fifties . . . Jonathan Rauch, "The Real Roots of Midlife Crisis," *The Atlantic*, December 2014.

About the Author

LESLEY STAHL is one of America's most recognized and experienced broadcast journalists. Her career has been marked by political scoops, surprising features and award-winning foreign reporting. She has been a *60 Minutes* correspondent since 1991; the 2015–16 season marks her twenty-fifth on the broadcast. Prior to joining *60 Minutes*, Stahl served as CBS News White House correspondent during the Carter, Reagan, and part of the George H. W. Bush presidencies. She also hosted *Face the Nation* from 1983 to 1991 and coanchored *America Tonight* from 1989 to 1990. She is married to author and screenwriter Aaron Latham. They have one daughter and two granddaughters.